A Manual for Long-Term Care Facilities

The Problem/Need-Oriented Approach to Planning and Evaluating Patient Care

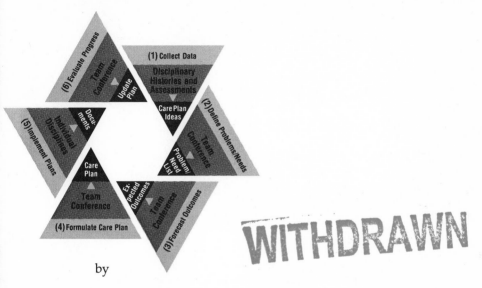

by

Leo Goldberg
Executive Administrator
Gold Medallion Nursing Centers
Minneapolis, Minnesota

Carolyn Benoit, R.N.
Consultant
Gold Medallion Nursing Centers

Carol Docken, T.R.S.
Consultant
Gold Medallion Nursing Centers

Earl Hoagberg
Coordinator, Special Projects
Gold Medallion Nursing Centers

Janet Wesselman, R.D.
Consultant
Gold Medallion Nursing Centers

Medallion
Communications

First edition.

Library of Congress Catalog Card Number: 78-70464

International Standard Book Number: 0-932822-01-0

Printed in the United States of America.

Contents

Acknowledgements

This book presents a health care system for long-term care facilities (LTCF's) based on Dr. Lawrence Weed's problem-oriented medical record (POMR). Although our version varies somewhat, it will quickly become apparent that we are indebted to Dr. Weed and to others who have built on his ideas. Perhaps this debt will be partially repaid if our book helps advance POMR principles into the long-term care sector of the health delivery system.

This is a "how to" manual. It distills experience acquired over five years of trial and error in developing a problem/need-oriented patient management system. We gladly recognize the contributions made during that time by many Gold Medallion professionals who helped us work out a practical system. Three former consultants played active roles in fashioning the ideas and procedures described in the manual: Margaret Maynard, R.D., Stella Townsend, R.R.A., and Jory Rasmussen, M.S.W. Gretchen Porter, our consulting nurse practitioner, deserves special mention for the case material and for her general counsel. Barbara Clawson helped in dozens of ways to make sure that the final manuscript was ready on time.

One delightful benefit of a project like this is that it brings closer contact with knowledgeable clinicians who share a commitment to improving the patient care process. We are especially grateful to friends who reviewed our manuscript and gave us the benefit of their insights and experience: Faye Abdellah, R.N., Ph.D., former director of the Office of Long Term Care, Department of Health, Education and Welfare; Howard Corbus, M.D., and Laura Swanson, R.N., coauthors of a recently published book* on the use of the POMR in nursing homes; and Mary Kay Hunt, R.D.,

---

*Adopting the Problem-Oriented Medical Record in Nursing Homes. Wakefield, Mass., Contemporary Publishing, Inc., 1978.

Course Coordinator, Continuing Education, Sister Kenny Institute, Minneapolis. The comments and suggestions of these generous reviewers are appreciated, although responsibility for the manual's contents rests solely with the authors.

Finally, we would like to acknowledge the continuing support and encouragement of Reynold P. Flom, M.D., President of Gold Medallion Nursing Centers, whose vision and commitment to leadership in long-term care have inspired our efforts.

Introduction

In the past, the pursuit of excellence in health care was reason enough for most long-term care facilities (LTCF's) to examine the merits of the problem/need-oriented system to be described here. Today, there is also strong external pressure to do so. The thrust of both existing and proposed legislation is to mandate quality care by prescribed standards and structured systems designed to facilitate assessment of the care process and its outcome in individual patients. Legislators and regulators appear to be leaning toward some type of problem/need-oriented system that emphasizes:

- Patient appraisal, including the definition of specific patient problems and needs.

- Setting measurable goals or expected outcomes.

- Developing and implementing concrete plans to achieve those goals and outcomes.

- Maintaining systematic records that ease the monitoring and assessment of the care process and its outcome.

Clearly, then, the challenge facing long-term health care providers is the *immediate* implementation of a system that accomplishes these objectives. Should providers delay in determining how they will define, evaluate, and assure quality care, they may be compelled to accept a system that complicates the provision of care without improving its quality.

This manual has been prepared to help meet that challenge. The product of several years' experimentation and hard work, it describes a health care system for LTCF's that is based on Dr. Weed's problem-oriented medical record (POMR).

Our search for a more effective means of providing quality patient care was motivated by our longtime interest in developing concepts, processes, and resources that are compatible with the unique mission of long-term care. Generally, LTCF's are modeled after acute-care hospitals, despite the belief that it is an inappropriate model. Our struggle to evolve a more suitable model finds expression in the term "integrated patient care," the foundation of the problem/need-oriented system of care outlined in this manual.

Integrated patient care means caring for the whole person. More than that, it means creating a climate in which every employee, every activity, every program, and even the facility itself reflect a genuine respect and concern for patients, staff members, and visiting families and friends. It means a concern for quality of life. This environment promotes health, fosters mental and social well-being, and encourages involvement in daily activities. What is more, staff members working in this environment begin to think of their jobs as a satisfying and rewarding part of life rather than as just a series of chores.

In other words, integrated patient care is a philosophy of care in which the patient is the focus of everything the LTCF is and does. It's objectives include:

- Broadening each staff member's perspective from a narrow concern for some special facet of the patient's needs to an appreciation for the patient as a whole person.

- Helping all staff members to develop their communication skills, improve their knowledge of human behavior, and increase their competence to function within an interdisciplinary team.

- Developing integrated programs of care to meet each patient's unique needs—physical, emotional, social, and spiritual—by pooling the insights, experience and efforts of all staff members.

- Establishing and maintaining constructive relationships with patients and their families to gain increased insight into patients' needs and to facilitate understanding and support of the facility's goals.

As these objectives suggest, implementing an integrated program of patient care is a large undertaking. Our problem/need-oriented system of care, although only a part of that larger program, can go a long way toward making integrated patient care a reality in any LTCF.

Leo Goldberg, Executive Administrator
Gold Medallion Nursing Centers

CHAPTER 1: An Overview of the Problem/Need-Oriented System in Long-Term Care

Although Dr. Weed originally designed the POMR as a teaching tool for medical students and as a means of enhancing the quality of care, its principles and techniques have been successfully adapted in many different health care settings. With appropriate modification, they are admirably suited for long-term care.

Simply stated, the problem/need-oriented system takes the problem-solving techniques used in everyday life and applies them to health care in the long-term care setting. It does so by means of a logical sequence of six action steps (see figure) that begins with information gathering, proceeds through problem/need definition and the formulation of expected outcomes and appropriate intervention plans, and ends with the actual provision of care and its systematic recording. At regular intervals, or whenever the patient's condition warrants it, the patient's status and care plan are reviewed and, if necessary, revised. The system supplies a simple method for organizing and documenting patient information, but its fundamental objective is to integrate, rationalize, and thus, improve quality of care by orienting the care process around the patient's defined problems/ needs.

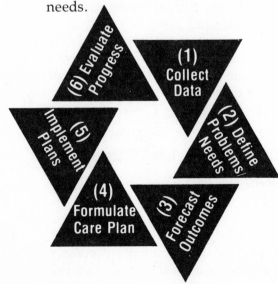

This six-step process varies somewhat from the conventional POMR. This is so because of the important differences between acute care and long-term care. These differences have to do with the multiple problems and extended stays characteristic of long-term patients which, in turn, shape the unique mission, philosophy, and organization of the LTCF. Thus, LTCF's employ various specialists who combine their skills to assess patients' needs and to plan, provide, and evaluate interventions aimed at resolving their problems, fulfilling their needs, and generally assuring their quality of life. This context of long-term care is reflected in three features of the present system of care:

- **Interdisciplinary team approach.** Although each discipline assesses and cares for the patient from its own perspective, each step of the problem/need-oriented system is an interdisciplinary process to assure coordinated effort and optimal outcomes.

- **Attention to the patient's comprehensive needs.** Physical care problems are addressed, but equal attention is given to routine health maintenance needs, life-style preferences, and general quality of life.

- **Periodic reviews of the patient's progress toward expected outcomes.** In some cases, restorative goals are set; more often, outcomes are determined for actions aimed at preventing or palliating illness or at maintaining health. In either case, these interrelated goals and expected outcomes are reviewed periodically. They are the only criteria by which the patient's progress can be assessed.

The Six Steps of the Problem/Need-Oriented System

Step 1. Developing the data base. The problem/need-oriented method begins with the gathering of specific information about the patient's past and current status by each discipline providing patient care. The initial data base includes both historic and assessment information. Sources and types of information included are shown below.

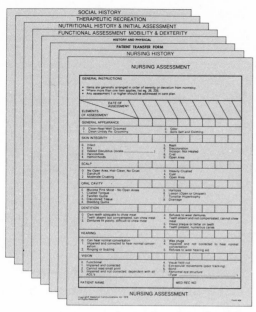

It is important that all disciplines involved in patient care help gather the data base to insure its comprehensiveness. The goal is to obtain a composite patient profile from many perspectives. Each discipline gathers historical and assessment information relevant to its own area of expertise. Summaries of this data base information are discussed during the care conference. The data base is constantly updated and expanded as new information comes to light or as the patient's condition changes.

Step 2. Defining the problem/need list. The data base is the foundation for defining the problem/need list, one of the most crucial steps in the process. The quality of the care plan and of the care rendered depends on the quality of effort invested in this step. This numbered list: **(1)** contains all problems/needs that concern the patient and care providers; **(2)** is expressed in terms supported by the data base; and **(3)** serves as the organizational index for each health record.

The problem/need list consists of two separate categories: **(1)** conventional problems and **(2)** patient needs that, if not met, could precipitate problems.

Conventional problems include any condition where the patient requires assistance to attain or maintain an optimal level of wellness, whether physical, social, mental or emotional. Examples are specific diagnoses, states of mind, abnormal laboratory findings, and pain. Also included are problems controlled by medication, diet, or appliances (e.g., hypertension, anxiety, impaired vision). The only exceptions are acute self-limiting problems (e.g., head colds). Such short duration problems are dealt with immediately and are recorded on a separate form to avoid making the problem/need list too unwieldy.

3

*

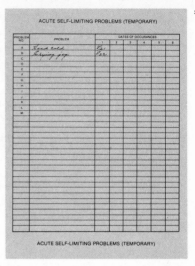

Patient needs include routine health maintenance needs, life-style preferences, and leisure needs (e.g., a desire to maintain former leisure patterns).

Step 3. Forecasting expected outcomes. In step 3, the patient care team evaluates the extent to which each defined problem/need can be resolved or controlled and forecasts the outcome that can be expected with optimal interventions. Team members should, however, avoid thinking that *they* must do everything for the patient. Rather, the team must view the patient holistically, considering not only the patient's problems and their interrelatedness but also the patient's specific or unique strengths and resources. Indeed, a patient's strengths—general vigor, motivation, intelligence—and such other resources as the interest and cooperation of family and friends will have a bearing on expected outcomes. Those outcomes will also be shaped by the team's experience with similar problems/needs and by available resources for intervention. Expected outcomes become the focus of the interventions planned in step 4 and serve as the criteria for evaluating the patient's progress in step 6.

Step 4. Formulating the care plan. Team members collaborate in step 4 to fashion a specific care program that will accomplish the expected outcomes determined in step 3. They list specific interventions and decide how each team member and the patient can contribute to or support the

---

*NOTE: Forms illustrated can be found in appendixes 1 and 2.

team's efforts. As shown below, the care plan for each problem/need consists of three separate elements (Dx, Rx, and Ed):

Dx. Plans for gathering additional diagnostic data to define or clarify the problem/need or to accurately chart the patient's status.

Rx. Intervention plans.

Ed. Educational plans to help patients (and their families) understand the purpose of each intervention, to encourage their involvement, and to instruct in self-care.

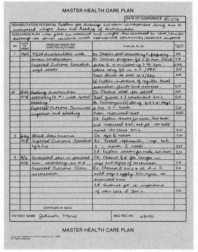

The master care plan also includes two general appraisals: **(1)** an initial statement of rehabilitation potential (in addition to a similar statement required of the physician) and **(2)** an initial statement of discharge potential. Both are the team's estimation of the patient's probable progress. These initial appraisals must be updated as the patient's status changes.

The master health care plan (i.e., problems, needs, expected outcomes, plans, and statements of rehabilitation and discharge potential) is recorded during the conference and placed in the chart.

Step 5. Implementing the plan and recording progress. In step 5, the care plan is executed and all clinical actions, observations, and patient reactions and responses are systematically recorded. These data are documented in flow sheets and progress notes. Progress notes are numbered to correspond with the related problem/need. These progress notes and flow sheets provide a record of specific treatments, interventions, side effects, or status changes, and can be readily followed by everyone concerned.

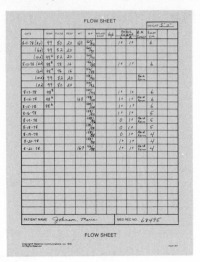

Progress notes are entered into the record as subjective, objective, assessment, and plan (SOAP) elements. These progress notes prove valuable for:

■ Documenting services provided.

■ Recording information and observations gathered during care.

■ Assessing changes in the patient's status.

■ Evaluating results.

■ Documenting the patient's reactions to care.

■ Serving as the basis for revising and updating the problem/need list, expected outcomes, and care plan.

■ Charting the patient's progress toward specified goals.

■ Indicating the persons accountable for providing individual elements of care.

Step 6. Reviewing and revising the care plan. The sixth and final step involves reviewing progress toward expected outcomes and, when necessary, revising the problem list, expected outcomes, or care plan. This evaluation is based on information in the progress notes and can be activated by:

■ The development of a new problem.

■ A marked change in the patient's condition.

■ The patient's failure to progress toward goals.

■ The facility's schedule for periodic review of care plans.

Although the review and revision procedure generally follows steps 1 through 4, the emphasis can vary.

The Advantages of the Problem/Need-Oriented System

Based on our experience, the problem/need-oriented system offers LTCF's many advantages in planning, providing, and evaluating patient care. For example:

- A problem/need list is essential to help manage long-term patients and prevent conflicts in treatment because long-term patients usually have multiple problems and ongoing primary health needs.

- Identifying the patient's problems/needs encourages consideration of their interrelatedness and relative importance, focuses attention on the whole person, and emphasizes the continuity and coordination of care.

- Defining the patient's problems/needs facilitates predicting outcomes, setting realistic goals, and developing appropriate plans to achieve them.

- Providing care becomes more meaningful because each specific aspect of the care plan is directly related to a particular problem/need and expected outcome.

- Understanding the reasons for actions motivates staff members and aids them in evaluating the effectiveness of interventions and the patient's progress toward expected outcomes.

- Using the numbered problem/need list as the index for organizing information provides a systematic, logical arrangement for auditing records.

- SOAP progress notes offer an attractive, meaningful alternative to traditional narrative notes, which tend to be redundant, trivial, inefficient, and obscure.

- The patient is the true focus of care because her or his concerns are always taken seriously and she or he is deliberately drawn into the care process.

CHAPTER 2: Interdisciplinary Patient Care Planning: The Vital First Step

Interdisciplinary patient care planning is an essential part of the problem/need-oriented system in long-term care. Many LTCF's, of course, already have such programs because patient care planning is desirable in itself and does not depend on the simultaneous adoption of the problem/need-oriented approach. The opposite, however, is *not* true: Problem/need-oriented patient care *does* rely on interdisciplinary patient care planning and cannot succeed without a vigorous planning conference program.

What is an Interdisciplinary Patient Care Planning Conference?

Casual observers might conclude that planning conferences are nothing more than a group of staff members talking about helping their patients. Although this impression is correct, in the problem/need-oriented system planning conferences are a much more structured, systematic process.

An interdisciplinary patient care planning conference is a regularly scheduled meeting in which staff members systematically review each patient to:

- Identify all specific problems and unique needs.
- Assess the patient's rehabilitation potential and define realistic short-term goals and expected outcomes to optimize physical and social functioning.
- Devise a comprehensive care program to achieve those goals and expectations, including specific plans for each identified problem/need.

Perhaps the patient care planning conference can be better explained by looking briefly at its various elements. First, the planning conference is a regularly scheduled meeting. Planning patient care programs is too important to be left to chance or to be fitted in as time permits. It must be given top priority and a specific day and hour is set aside for regular meetings.

Second, regular meetings at frequent intervals are essential if plans are to be promptly made and implemented for each newly admitted patient, each patient whose condition significantly changes, and patients whose care plans are scheduled for periodic review. The conference must be held seven to ten days after a patient is admitted, although immediately upon admission nursing service and other disciplines caring for the patient prepare preliminary care plans based on data from the transfer form, the physician's orders, and their initial assessments. Revision conferences are scheduled as soon as possible after significant changes are noted. The master care plans of all patients must be reviewed by the team quarterly.

Third, the planning conference participants are staff members directly involved in the care of patients to be discussed. Although good care plans are based on understanding the patient and his or her needs as fully as possible, most individuals tend to have a limited picture of others.

- *How* we see others and *what* we see or fail to see are strongly influenced by personal feelings and past experience, which can give us incomplete and sometimes inaccurate impressions.

- Patients relate differently to different staff members for similar reasons and often disclose more of themselves and their feelings to one person than to another.

- Busy staff members tend to see patients from the standpoint of their areas of expertise instead of seeing the whole person.

It is more likely that the patient's problems/needs can be fully understood and successfully addressed when all those who provide care pool their insights and information. Thus, an interdisciplinary conference brings together representatives from the various services—nursing, dietary, social work, physical therapy, occupational therapy, therapeutic recreation, volunteers—and other helping professions (e.g., the clergy).

Fourth, the planning process involves a well-defined, systematic series of steps—the problem/need-oriented system.

Establishing an Interdisciplinary Planning Conference Program

The unique needs and resources of each LTCF will determine how to develop interest in, and initiate, a planning conference program. The suggestions outlined here are applicable to most situations but may need modification to fit particular circumstances. The one essential ingredient is the interest and commitment of the administrator and department supervisors and their determination to make the program work.

Begin by interesting key leaders. Talk with them about sections of this manual, particularly those describing integrated patient care, the problem/need-oriented system, and the patient care planning conference. Most important changes are wrought by one or two enthusiastic persons who persist in their efforts to educate and influence colleagues about ideas that have captured their imagination. When enough leaders are interested, *form an ad hoc committee to implement the program.*

The ad hoc committee should familiarize itself with the mechanics of problem/need-oriented care and interdisciplinary patient care planning. Study this manual and discuss the details of the program. Confer with long-term care providers who are already using the system. Take advantage of seminars or workshops on problem/need-oriented patient care.

The ad hoc committee should *visualize the program in terms of specific needs and resources.* These are some questions that need answers:

- How many patients are admitted in an average month? How often do their conditions change significantly? At what intervals are care plans routinely reviewed? What does this information suggest about the frequency and duration of planning conference meetings?
- In terms of usual work flow, what day and time are best for scheduling planning meetings? What is the most suitable meeting place?

11

■ What revisions of the present patient record system will be necessary? How will the necessary forms be obtained or developed?

■ Which staff members have the qualifications and leadership abilities to effectively lead the planning conference team?

■ Who are the "key" staff members whose support will assure the program's success? How can they be drawn into the program most effectively?

■ Which staff members are likely to resist or oppose the program and why? What effect will this have on the attitudes of others? How can their support be won or their opposition neutralized? If they continue to oppose the change, what action should be taken?

■ What is the best way to introduce the program to the staff and to prepare them for informed involvement? When should the program be unveiled?

Having worked through these questions, the committee should be ready to proceed. *The best qualified persons should then be enlisted to conduct and implement the program.* Since leadership is the key to a successful program, it is important to consider the job descriptions and qualifications.

Conference team leader. Success hinges to a great extent on the skills and abilities of the conference team leader. It is important to choose the most qualified person early in the planning stage and closely involve him or her in implementing the program. Although the conference team leader may be a professional nurse, other competent professional staff should not be overlooked. The team leader's *personal* qualities are just as important as her or his professional qualifications, since the team leader will set the tone for the entire care team. The person chosen must be able to:

■ Lead without dominating the team's deliberations.

■ Both teach and learn from co-workers, sharing personal expertise without being patronizing and being just as willing to learn from others.

12

- Recognize and help resolve any interpersonal conflicts that could impair the team's effectiveness.
- "Draw out" team members who hesitate to take part with non-threatening encouragement.
- Restrain team members who dominate the team's discussion without alienating them.

When selecting the conference team leader, the committee should also be aware of the duties of the position:

- Helping to plan and implement the problem/need-oriented system and the planning conference program.
- Selecting and being familiar with the patients to be discussed at each planning conference meeting.
- Encouraging the involvement of all team members.
- Summing up the team's discussion in a coherent plan.
- Designating team members to do the necessary recording.

Conference coordinator. The conference team leader is busy with assigned duties and should not be further burdened with the routine aspects of the program. So, someone with clerical skills and initiative (e.g., the health records manager) should be designated to serve as the conference coordinator. The duties of the coordinator are to:

- Notify team members about scheduled planning meetings and the patient agenda.
- Check on the availability and presentability of the meeting room.
- Make sure the necessary materials and equipment are available at meeting time.

Another essential preparatory task for the ad hoc committee is *revising its current health care record system to conform with the problem/need-oriented system.* It is easier to use commercially available forms initially than to design your own forms. The major forms, the uses of which are described in chapter 3, are:

13

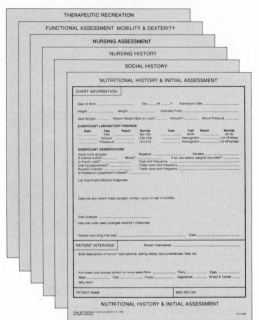

Patient history and assessment forms. These separate forms for each discipline are part of the data base and included in the patient's health record.

Patient care conference preparation worksheet. A working tool used by each conference participant which is destroyed following each meeting.

Problem/need list. This chart form displays the patient's numbered problems/needs and serves as an index for all charted information.

Master health care plan. This chart form lists each numbered problem/need, expected outcome, care plan, and initial statements of rehabilitation and discharge potential.

14

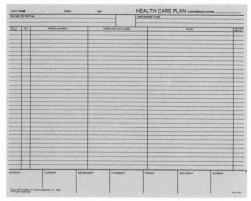

Health care plan. This is a penciled desktop (i.e., visible file) version of the patient's problem list and care plan.

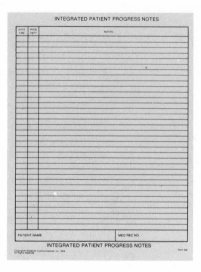

Integrated patient progress notes. SOAP notes are recorded on this chart form.

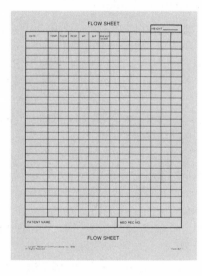

Flow sheet. This chart form documents measurable data and observations.

Another preparatory task for the ad hoc committee is to *decide on a meeting schedule.* Here are four useful guidelines:

(1) Estimate the number of patients requiring care planning during an average month. Add to this an estimate of the number of patients whose conditions can be expected to change enough to warrant care plan revision in an average month.

(2) Calculate the total time needed each week for conferences. Experienced teams spend 45 to 60 minutes per patient on initial health care plans.

(3) Generally, planning conference meetings should not exceed 60 to 90 minutes because efficiency declines as meetings lengthen. In addition, since learning the conference process is of prime importance, fewer patients should be scheduled at the first few meetings.

(4) After considering the daily work flow and consulting with department supervisors and team members, choose a regular meeting time and stick to it!

It is essential that the ad hoc committee *prepare the staff for the new program.* All staff members should attend inservice meetings and team members should be prepared for their roles on the planning conference team. These three suggestions may prove helpful:

(1) Keep key staff members informed during the planning stage. It is always easier to win acceptance and cooperation for a new program when those who will be affected have some knowledge of the program and are involved in setting it up.

(2) A week or two before the program starts, hold an informal staff meeting to inform all staff members about the inception and details of the program. One simple message should come through: "Our facility is beginning an important new direction in patient care. We want all of you to know about it and to be a part of the program."

(3) Use the first scheduled meeting as an orientation session for the team. Proficiency is acquired as team members gain experience. The objectives of the first meeting are to:

- Create interest and enthusiasm.
- Promote a spirit of teamwork.
- Provide team members with a general understanding of the process and their roles.
- Give team members firsthand planning experience.

(6) Evaluate Progress

Team Conference

Update Plan

(1) Collect Data

Disciplinary Histories and Assessments

Care Plan Ideas

(2) Define Problems/Needs

Team Conference

Problem/ Need List

Documents

Individual Disciplines

(5) Implement Plans

Care Plan

Team Conference

(4) Formulate Care Plan

Expected Outcomes

Team Conference

(3) Forecast Outcomes

CHAPTER 3: Problem/Need-Oriented Patient Care In Action: Steps 1 Through 5

This chapter provides a "cookbook" approach to implementing the problem/need-oriented system using a typical patient to illustrate the process. The table below portrays the steps of this process to be discussed, together with the various specific tasks and methods or tools involved in carrying out those steps. (Review and revision of care plans, step 6, will be discussed in the following chapter.)

STEPS	TASKS	METHODS/TOOLS
Preparatory Activity—performed by each individual discipline		
Step 1	■ Interview patient ■ Assess patient ■ Analyze *all* data ■ Prepare care plan ideas	■ History form ■ Assessment form ■ Preparation Worksheet (1) Background Summary Column (2) Problem/Need Column ■ Preparation Worksheet (1) Expected Outcome Column (2) Plan Column
Planning Conference Activity—performed by the interdisciplinary team		
Step 2	■ Verbal summaries of background information relevant to care planning ■ Team agrees on completeness of problem/need list ■ Title, arrange, & number problems/needs	■ Team leader lists problems on chalkboard as they are identified ■ Team leader modifies chalkboard list as necessary ■ Team leader modifies chalkboard list as necessary ■ Problem/Need List recorded by scribe
Step 3	■ Prepare rehabilitation potential statement & initial discharge plan	■ Team leader writes on chalkboard ■ Designated scribes record in Master Health Care Plan & Visible Record Health Plan

STEPS	TASKS	METHODS/TOOLS
Step 3 *(continued)*	■ Agree on expected outcome statement for Problem No. 1	■ Team leader writes on chalkboard ■ Scribes record on Master Health Care Plan & Visible Record Health Plan
	■ Agree on care plan for Problem No. 1	■ Team leader writes on chalkboard ■ Scribes record on Master Health Care Plan & Visible Record Health Plan
	■ Repeat above process (i.e., agree on (1) expected outcome and (2) care plan) for each remaining problem/need	■ Team leader erases expected outcome & plan for Problem 1 and repeats the process for each succeeding problem. ■ Scribes record on Master Health Care Plan & Visible Record Health Plan
Step 4	■ If patient was not present, decide how, and by whom, the plan will be shared with the patient	■ Team leader assigns responsibility
	■ Decide if family conference is indicated	■ Team leader assigns responsibility

Followup Activity—performed by the interdisciplinary team

Step 5	■ Hold patient/family conferences	
	■ Carry out plan and record progress	■ SOAP notes ■ Flow sheets

Preparing for the Patient Care Planning Conference

Arranging the patient agenda. Five to seven days before the scheduled planning conference, the team leader prepares the patient agenda. If there are more patients than can be conferenced in the allotted time, the list is prioritized and additional meetings are planned. Generally, priority is determined as follows: (1) newly admitted patients in the order of admission, and (2) patients whose condition has changed and for whom a revision of the problem/need list and care plan is indicated.

Notifying team members. The conference coordinator reminds each team member about the meeting time five to seven days before the meeting, and gives them the patient agenda. One good way to do this is by providing each team member with a set of preparation worksheets filled in with the names of patients to be conferenced. The meeting notice and patient agenda are also posted at this time. Prior to the meeting, the coordinator also checks on the availability and presentability of the meeting room, and makes sure that the necessary materials and equipment are present at meeting time.

Besides the team leader, other potential planning conference participants are: the director of nursing or charge nurse or both, nursing assistant(s) assigned to care for the patients scheduled for discussion, dietitian or dietetic service supervisor, therapeutic recreation coordinator, occupational therapist, physical therapist, social worker, housekeeping supervisor, and personnel from other relevant specialties (e.g., psychologist, speech therapist, volunteer coordinator, and clergy).

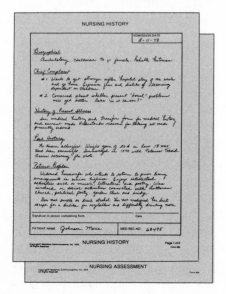

Collecting the data base. A defined data base is collected for each patient scheduled for discussion as individual team members interview and assess these patients prior to the meeting. Thus, the use of structured assessment forms is strongly recommended because such forms provide a systematic means for gathering and assessing information, observations, and insights relevant to each team member's particular discipline. During

21

this process, team members consult transfer forms and other medical records, but they rely chiefly on patient (and family) interviews and their own assessments. The focus of each team member varies with his or her area of expertise.

Using the preparation worksheet. Using the preparation worksheet, each team member also prepares for the meeting by identifying *all* of the patient's problems/needs, not just those that seem to be relevant to his or her area of diagnostic expertise. Then each team member decides on a reasonable outcome for each identified problem/need and develops preliminary ideas on how her or his discipline can be most effective in helping to achieve those outcomes. Merely working tools, the preparation worksheets are *not* incorporated into the patient's record, but are destroyed following the meeting.

Preparation by each team member cannot be overstressed. Lack of preparation is by far the most important cause of the failures and inadequacies of patient care planning and is unfair to both patients and co-workers.

The Patient Care Planning Conference

The four main steps of the patient care planning conference are: **(1)** discussing the data base, **(2)** defining the problem/ need list, **(3)** forecasting expected outcomes, and **(4)** formulating the master health care plan. A fictional, newly admitted patient will be used in this section to illustrate the care planning process. The task is to develop an *initial* care program which will be reviewed periodically and revised as needed.

22

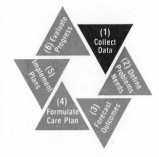

Step 1. Discussing the data base. The objective is to discuss information about the patient's health care profile to enable the team to define all of the patient's problems/needs. Thus, each team member verbally summarizes data base information he has collected beforehand, presenting those elements not already presented by others that are relevant to identifying the patient's problems/needs and to planning a realistic care program. The team leader does *not* prepare a patient assessment, but must be familiar with the patient. The team leader is responsible for pacing the meeting by:

- Asking team members to limit oral summaries to one or two minutes.

- Allowing time for brief questions and answers but postponing lengthier discussions that are not directly relevant to the team's job.

- Making sure that the patient's chart is available.

- Using a blackboard to list the patient's problems/needs as they are mentioned during this phase of the meeting.

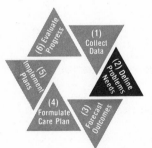

Step 2. Defining the master problem/need list. The objective is to develop a permanent numbered list of all problems/needs, expressed in terms supported by the data base. Using the preparation worksheet, each team member already has begun to list the patient's problems as she or he perceives them. In preparing for the meeting, the team leader also will have identified and listed the patient's problems/needs. His or her task is to guide the team in consolidating a master problem/need list. The team leader will find it helpful to:

- Write all suggested problems/needs on a blackboard to keep the list before the team. This minimizes redundancy and enhances the team's understanding of interrelationships between the problems/needs.
- Encourage each team member to discuss, assess, and help organize the master problem/need list.
- Keep the meeting on schedule by allowing about ten minutes for this step.

Types of problems/needs included on the master problem/ need list are:

- Specific medical diagnoses, e.g., hypertension.
- Specific nursing diagnoses, e.g., depletion of body fluids.
- Symptoms, e.g., leg pain.
- Mental impairment, e.g., disorientation.
- Abnormal laboratory findings, e.g., low hemoglobin level.
- Risks, e.g., heavy reliance on cigarettes.
- Functional limitations, e.g., inability to walk independently secondary to CVA.
- Sensory deficits, e.g., blindness.
- Allergies, e.g., reaction to penicillin.
- Psychological problems, e.g., reactive depression following the death of a spouse.
- Social problems, e.g., does not initiate conversation with residents or staff.
- Leisure problems, e.g., inability to resume former leisure patterns secondary to CVA.
- Primary health needs.
- Leisure needs, e.g., desires to participate in musical activity.
- Economic or financial needs, e.g., insolvency.
- Life-style preferences.

Contrary to some opinions, it is recommended that medical diagnoses be included in the master problem/need list. Their inclusion:

- Provides professionals with language which relates signs and symptoms.
- Acknowledges the physician's role (i.e., the absentee team member) on the care team by using language with which he communicates, thereby facilitating monitoring and progress note writing by the doctor.
- Helps identify causes, or the need to uncover causes, for any new signs or symptoms that may develop.
- Facilitates medical care evaluation studies by providing more clearly identified, more easily retrievable data.
- Makes the physician's orders understandable as they relate to medically diagnosed problems.

The care team's primary responsibility is to define problems and needs in terms of its present level of understanding. This means avoiding guesswork or presumptive medical diagnoses. Thus, if a hemoglobin level is too low but the physician has not diagnosed anemia, the problem should be titled "low hemoglobin," not "anemia." Similarly, "frequent crying" is a legitimate problem title, and the team should avoid assuming that it is caused by depression. In both examples, one element of the care plan would be to acquire additional information to clarify the underlying nature or cause of the problems.

To organize the master problem/need list, proceed as follows:

(1) List the patient's *physical problems* and group those problems that are related. Begin with diagnoses and information contained in the transfer form and other medical records. Here are some *guidelines*:

- List each diagnosed problem, followed by its physical, functional, or behavioral manifestation(s) that require care and management.

25

1	562.1 564.0	*Mild diverticulosis with chronic constipation*	*1965*		*
5	401	*Hypertension with intermittent mild ankle edema*	*1975*		

- Should a diagnosed problem manifest itself in more than one way and require a different care plan, treat such manifestations as separate problems, with the notation that they are secondary to a previously numbered problem.

2	562.1 569.2	*Resolving diverticulitis secondary to # 1 with rectal bleeding*	*July 1978*		
3		*Blood loss anemia secondary to # 2*	*July '78*		
4	918	*Excoriated skin in perianal area secondary to #2*	*8/6/78*		

- Indicate other physical problems or functional disabilities, if any.

8	374.9	*Immature bilateral cataracts*	*Feb '78*		
9	454.9	*Varicosities, both legs*	*P.T.A.*		

- Include problems controlled by means of medication, diet, or appliances.

10	525.0	*Edentulous*	*PTA*		

- Resolved past problems are not to be included, although major past problems should be noted in the patient's history.

(2) List the patient's *routine health maintenance needs.* The objective here is to anticipate and provide for periodic prophylactic and diagnostic procedures, the omission of which could give rise to serious health problems. NOTE: specific procedures are listed in the care plan, *not* on the problem/need list.

14		*Primary health needs*			

*All examples are taken from the sample problem/need list found in Appendix 1.

(3) List any *social, behavioral, or leisure-related problems* not already listed. Some social and behavioral problems may have been listed earlier because of their relationship to certain physical problems.

(4) List the patient's *life-style preferences*. The objective is to identify and provide for unique patient desires that will enrich the patient's life and support optimal physical and psychosocial health. NOTE: specifics are listed in the care plan, *not* on the problem/need list.

The master problem/need list is placed at the front of the patient's health record as an index for that record. The list is *not* static, but requires updating in circumstances like these:

■ Problems sometimes will be retitled as the team's knowledge of the problem increases.

Old Title: "Low hemoglobin"
  New Title: "Blood loss anemia."
Old Title: "Refuses participation in all activities other than intraindividual"
  New Title: "Fears inability to meet psychomotor expectations of staff."

■ New problems will arise that must be added to the master list and numbered sequentially.

■ As problems become inactive or are resolved, they are *not* dropped from the master list but the date of inactivity or resolution is noted in the inactive column.

Remember, acute self-limiting problems are not included on the master problem/need list. These temporary or short-term (less than ten days) problems, such as head colds, stomach flu, and "crying jags," are listed separately to

27

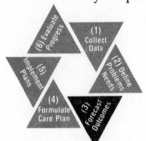

ACUTE SELF-LIMITING PROBLEMS (TEMPORARY)

avoid making the master list too un-wieldly and to facilitate monitoring their frequency. They are assigned an alphabetical "number" to prevent confusion. Each occurrence of an acute self-limiting problem is noted and dated, because repeated episodes of the same problem may suggest a more serious underlying problem. In such cases, the temporary problem may be placed on the master list.

Step 3. Forecasting expected outcomes. The forecasting of reasonable expectations or out-comes for each problem/need is necessary if intervention planning is to have a focus (step 4) and if the evaluation of patient progress is to be done against a meaningful criterion (step 6).

There are four principal types of expected outcomes: **(1)** restoration, **(2)** maintenance, **(3)** prevention, and **(4)** palliation. The term "goal" connotes restoration of health or function, but is applicable to only a fraction of the problems encountered in long-term care. The majority involve outcomes such as maintaining health and existing functional levels and preventing or palliating illness. Good care planning begins with the team's careful estimation of realistic outcomes for each problem/need.

Patients often have strengths and resources that can influence the outcome of the care process. Experienced planning teams avoid assuming that *they* must do every-thing for the patient and search for patient resources that can be marshalled to support the care process. The follow-ing checklist of potential patient resources, based on suggestions from the Council for Long-Term Care, Joint Commission on Accreditation of Hospitals, will help in in-ventorying and assessing these strengths:

- General health status—general vigor or robustness, stamina, good hygiene, concern about proper diet, good appetite.
- Mental resources—intelligence, alertness, curiosity, interest in reading and learning, good memory and attention span.
- Personality characteristics—emotional stability, determination, flexibility, tolerance for discomfort or pain, acceptance of and adjustment to limitations.
- Social skills—enjoyment of others, ability to initiate conversations, responsibility for others, general or particular interest in games, hobbies, and other activities.
- Spiritual strengths—a deep personal religious faith that imparts meaning to life and its events, a sense of personal worth and of being cared for, a sense of being nourished or sustained by prayer, preaching, or religious worship.
- Outside supportive strengths—competent, cooperative and interested family members or friends; representatives of social, fraternal, or work-related organizations; positive placement possibilities following discharge; membership in community organizations that can provide specialized help (e.g., Alcoholics Anonymous or colostomy or mended heart clubs).

When such strengths are identified, they should influence expected outcomes, be considered in care planning, and have a bearing on discharge plans and the statement of rehabilitation potential.

Good care planning begins with a careful assessment of each problem/need in the light of realistic and achievable outcomes which then become the measures of care plan effectiveness.* Writing good expected outcome statements takes thought and practice. There are *four essential elements:*

---

* Additional insights into the importance and skill of goal writing and analysis can be found in two books by Robert F. Mager: **Preparing Instructional Objectives** (1962) and **Goal Analysis** (1972). Both are published by Fearon Publishers, Belmont, California.

- The expected outcome must *describe specific and observable end results or patient behaviors*, such as physical changes, functional abilities, or behavioral changes. This element of the statement answers the question, what is to be achieved, or what will the patient be doing?

1	1965	Mild diverticulosis with
		chronic constipation
		Expected Outcome: Establish
		soft stools

- The expected outcome must *define the level of achievement that is expected in terms of measurable criteria*, such as physiological measures, laboratory values, or the frequency, duration, or extent to which the patient can perform expected behaviors. This element of the statement answers the question, how well is the outcome to be achieved?

5	1975	Hypertension c̄ intermittent
		mild ankle edema.
		Expected Outcome: Control BP
		to < 150/90 and eliminate
		ankle edema.

- The expected outcome should *also describe any special conditions of evaluation that may influence the end result or behavior*, such as assistive devices or compensatory equipment. This element of the statement answers the question, under what circumstances will the outcome be achieved?

8	Feb. 1978	Immature bilateral cataracts.
		Expected Outcome: Maintain
		independence in ADLs with
		the use of adaptive devices.

- When writing expected outcome statements involving attitudes, appreciations, or understandings, the statement must *include a single described behavior or set of behaviors that will indicate the presence of the alleged performance, and about which there would be general agreement*. This element of the statement should answer the question, what behavior(s) will indicate that this outcome has been achieved?

13	8/11	Expresses fear of becoming
	1978	dependent.
		Expected Outcome: Will feel
		comfortable c̄ limited depen-
		dence by asking family +
		staff for assistance as
		necessary.

In addition to these essential elements, good expected outcome statements have other important characteristics. For one thing, they are *understandable*, both to the patient and to the care team. Professional jargon, abbreviations, and symbols should be avoided for clarity and to minimize ambiguous interpretations.

10	PTA	Edentulous
		Expected Outcome: Maintain
		ability to chew meat.

When appropriate, expected outcomes *may include intermediate steps (or rates of progress)* to be reached in achieving a longer-range goal.

6	1976	Obesity
		Expected Outcome: Reduce wt.
		to 140# at rate of 1-2#/week

Finally, expected outcomes ought to be *challenging, but realistically achievable.* Unrealistic goals frustrate, rather than challenge, the care team. However, restoration of health or function should never be sacrificed in favor of maintaining existing health levels if the possibility of improvement is present.

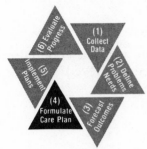

Step 4. Formulating the initial care plan. In the fourth stage of the planning process the team develops specific plans for achieving the expected outcomes that have just been defined. These plans are then integrated into a comprehensive program of care. Certain principles should govern this phase:

(A) In formulating the care plan, the team should *begin by evaluating existing plans before deciding on additional interventive measures.* Some elements of the care plan have already been determined, and these plans, together with ideas from the team members, form the "raw material" from which the initial care plan will be formed. The sequence commonly is:

  (1) The physician's orders are reviewed, related to the specific problems to which they apply, and incorporated into the care plan.

  (2) Plans previously initiated by nursing service and other departments are reviewed and evaluated before being included or discarded in favor of alternative approaches.

  (3) Additional suggestions by team members are discussed, evaluated, and included, modified, or discarded.

(B) *All plans—existing and proposed—should be evaluated against the patient's entire range of problems/needs and total life situation before they are incorporated into the plan.* Plans must be tailored to each patient's unique needs, strengths, and life-style. Any specific plan, no matter how ideal it may ordinarily be for dealing with a given problem, could be wholly inappropriate for some patients.

In developing the care plan, attention must be given to each of the three elements of the plan: **(1)** Dx, plans for gathering information about the problem; **(2)** Rx, plans for intervention; and **(3)** Ed, plans for educating patients and families.

Dx. These plans include all actions designed to obtain information needed to clarify the nature or origin of the patient's problems/needs or to chart his or her status. Included are laboratory tests, procedures for monitoring status, observations by team members, and plans for obtaining additional information from the patient's physician, relatives, transferring institution, consultants, and other sources. It is essential that information-gathering plans be described in specific detail and include:

- The tests or procedures to be done.

- The exact time or times that tests or procedures are to be performed.

- The name or initials of the staff person or position who is to perform the task.

2	July 1978	Resolving diverticulitis secondary to #1 with rectal bleeding.	Dx: Observe stool for blood Stool guaiac x 3 consecutive bm's	NA CN

- Any special instructions.

6	1976	Obesity Expected Outcome: Reduce wt. to 140# at rate of 1-2#/week	Dx: Weigh q̄ monday ā breakfast Observe between meal eating.	NA AS

- Findings "outside normal ranges" when appropriate, along with instructions about follow-up actions to be taken when abnormal values are found.

5	1975	Hypertension c̄ intermittent mild ankle edema. Expected Outcome: Control BP to <150/90 and eliminate ankle edema.	Dx: BP q̄ a.m. ℞ arm; call M.D. if >180/100. Check ankle edema q̄ d; notify M.D. if >2+	CN CN

- Special observations relevant to the team's expectations for the patient's specific condition.

4	8/6 1978	Excoriated skin in perianal area, secondary to #2. Expected Outcome: Clear excoriation.	Dx: Observe q d for changes in size and degree of excoriation.		CN

While the above mentioned guidelines are useful, the care team should avoid the pitfall of making its diagnostic plans too elaborate. It is not necessary to list every possible test, procedure, or observation; only those that are relevant to the specific patient under consideration need be included. For example, while *The Merck Manual** includes numerous tests, procedures, and observations that might be employed in diagnosing or monitoring patients with congestive heart failure, it is highly unlikely that care teams in long-term care facilities would include more than two or three of these approaches for any given patient.

Rx. Plans in this category include prescribed medications, nursing care orders, physical therapy, planned leisure activities, individual or group counseling, attitude therapy, and special diets. Characteristics and examples of good intervention plans are:

- Plans must be accurately described and include such specific details as dosage, strength, frequency and time of drug administration.

2	July 1978	Resolving diverticulitis secondary to #1 with rectal bleeding. Expected Outcome: Eliminate infection and bleeding.	Dx: Observe stool for blood Stool guaiac x 3 consecutive bm's Rx: Achromycin (0) 250 mg qid x 21 days 2 hrs. a.c. meals Fiber restricted diet	NA CN CN DSS

---

* **The Merck Manual of Diagnosis and Therapy.** Rahway, N.J., Merck & Co., Inc.

- Plans must include the name of the activity or procedure to be performed, the time and duration if relevant, and any special instructions.

7	July 1978	Mild anxiety secondary to #2	Rx: Valium 10 mg bid/PRN	CN
			Daily 1:1 Counseling to establish relationship of trust.	SW
			Passive friendliness by all staff; wait for pt. to make first move & respond accordingly.	AS

- Specific intervention plans must include the name or initials of the person or position who provides each specified intervention.

Ed. Patient and family education is a vital part of good care. Studies of patient compliance show that as many as 50 percent do not follow their doctors' orders because they do not understand the nature or gravity of the problem or the purpose of particular orders, are ignorant or uncertain about how orders should be carried out, and fail to understand or appreciate the importance of compliance. It is the care team's responsibility to overcome these barriers.

Authors of good care plans always consider the educational implications of each element of care to:
- Make sure patients understand the nature of the problem, each element of the care plan, and why it is being done.

6	1976	Obesity	Ed: Explain relationship of excess	
		Expected Outcome: Reduce wt	wt. to elevated BP, and importance	CN/DSS
		to 140# at rate of 1-2#/week	of following 1200 cal diet c̄ no high cal. snacks.	

- Equip patients to monitor their own status through self-observation.

2	July 1978	Resolving diverticulitis secondary to #1 with rectal bleeding.	Ed: Explain reasons for meds, lab tests, and restricted diet; ask pt. to call	
			nurse to check bm's.	CN
		Expected Outcome: Eliminate infection and bleeding.		

35

■ Teach patients the skills they need to function at higher levels.

9	PTa	Varicosities, both legs.	Ed: Instruct in avoiding tight garters,	
		Expected Outcome: Prevent	crossing legs, prolonged standing or sitting,	
		inflammation, stasis ulcer,	importance of reduced weight + correct	
		and discomfort.	procedure for putting on support hose.	CN

■ Enlist the cooperation of patients and families in helping achieve realistic goals.

5	1975	Hypertension c̄ intermittent	Ed: Explain reasons for Na-restricted	
		mild ankle edema.	diet & elevation of feet.	DSS/CN
		Expected Outcome: Control BP	Explain diet restrictions to family &	
		to < 150/90 and eliminate	discourage bringing in restricted food.	SW
		ankle edema.		

Initial discharge plan and rehabilitation potential/long-term goal statement. Initial health care plans also include an initial discharge plan and a rehabilitation potential/long-term goal statement. Both are based on the planning team's present state of knowledge about the patient's entire range of problems/needs, strengths and total life situation, present status, and probable progress in the long-term care facility. These are only preliminary judgments that may be revised to reflect later changes in the patient's status. A sample preliminary discharge plan is:

DISCHARGE PLAN When goals are attained and weight has decreased to 140#, consider discharge to prior residence with appropriate community resource support.

This discharge plan is conditioned on the attainment of goals set for the patient and implies the team's belief that these goals will be reached and that discharge is therefore possible.

In preparing the rehabilitation potential/long-term goal statement, the team should consider the physician's estimate of the patient's rehabilitation potential at admission. However, the statement represents the *team's* judgment about the probable functional level that can be achieved, in-

36

cluding the reasons supporting the team's judgment. A sample rehabilitation potential/long-term goal statement is:

REHABILITATION POTENTIAL *Excellent for discharge and return to independent living due to anticipated weight loss and healing of diverticulitis.*

Completing health records. The planning conference is a working session in which team members construct the care plan (i.e., the problem/need list, expected outcomes, and the care plan itself). The documents embodying these elements are completed *during* the planning meeting by individual team members assigned to these tasks.* (Remember, the team leader *never* becomes directly involved in these recording tasks, since conducting the meeting requires full-time attention.) It is both time-consuming and risky to delay the recording process until after the meeting. With practice, the problem/need list, master health care plan, and the visible file health plan can be accurately recorded during the meeting at a considerable savings in time.

The goal is to translate the team's efforts into working documents to guide and direct the team's daily activities. The documents systematically arrange the patient's problems/needs so that the purpose of each care element and its relationship to a particular problem/need and expected outcome can be seen at a glance and be easily understood. These working documents include:

(A) **Data base (history and assessment) forms.** Each discipline represented on the planning team has prepared a written data base (history and assessment) prior to the meeting, and presents its relevant highlights verbally during the meeting. These data base forms are incorporated into the patient's health record.

(B) **The master problem/need list.** This list serves as the index for the patient's entire health record. Its comple-

---

* At the beginning, however, it is probably wiser to delegate the recording task to a non-participating "scribe" in order to free team members to learn the care planning process. As the team becomes accustomed to the process, the recording function can be taken over by team members.

tion should be delegated to a team member who writes legibly and is familiar with medical terminology. The master problem/need list is compiled during the meeting and recorded on a special form. The form includes space for the number and title of each active problem/need and the date of onset. If the date is unknown, a note is made that onset was prior to admission (PTA).

(C) **The master health care plan.** Like the problem/need list, the master health care plan is recorded during the conference on a special form. The form includes space for:

- Personal data on the patient—name and medical record number.
- Date of the planning conference.
- Space for the rehabilitation potential/long-term goal statement.
- Space for the discharge plan.
- Separate columns for recording **(1)** the problem/need numbers, **(2)** dates of onset, **(3)** problem/need titles and expected outcomes, **(4)** care plans, (Dx, Rx, and Ed), and **(5)** accountability.

The master health care plan appears prior to the first page of the progress notes in the patient's health record, where it provides the baseline against which the patient's progress is measured.

(D) **The visible file health care plan.** A desk-top form of the master health care plan is prepared during the meeting for inclusion in the patient's visible file. (It is essential that this form be compatible with the problem/need-oriented system.) This form includes space for each numbered problem/need in one column along with its expected outcome, and the several care plan elements developed to deal with that problem listed in a parallel column. In addition, the form includes space for some of the information (i.e., personal, social, and physician's orders) usually found in this type of record. It is written in pencil to accommodate later changes. It is *not* a legal record.

This is perhaps a good place to reiterate that the problem/need-oriented care plan and record system has several distinct advantages over the conventional patient management system:

- There are fewer omissions and errors in patient management with the problem/need-oriented system, because orders and treatment plans are not listed haphazardly but are organized systematically around each specific problem/need.

- Staff members carry out orders more intelligently and with greater interest when they understand the reasons for, and probable outcomes of, specific orders and plans.

- It is easier to evaluate the effectiveness of specific plans and orders when their purpose and expected outcomes are clearly stated.

THE FOLLOW-UP

The work of the planning conference team becomes operational when it has been translated into an understandable working guide (i.e., the master health care plan), and when an attempt has been made to gain the active understanding and involvement of the patient and family in achieving realistic outcomes. Follow-up activities designed to implement the team's work involve: conferring with the patient (and sometimes the patient's family) about the plan and implementing the plan and recording progress (step 5).

Conferring with the patient about the plan. Clearly, patients must participate in the planning process because their involvement is vital to the team's understanding of their problems/needs, and to the development and implementation of care plans to meet those needs. Since patients must be fully aware of the plan and its objectives, they are: **(1)** always involved *before* the planning conference in the patient assessment process; **(2)** sometimes involved *during* all or part of the planning conference itself; and **(3)** always involved *after* the planning conference either by bringing the patient to the team or by designating a particular team member to confer with the patient about the care plan.

The finest care plan cannot be fully effective if the patient fails to understand it or is not involved in its implementation. Since understanding and active involvement depend on knowledge, a post-planning conference with the patient is essential. The care plan, the reasons and expectations underlying each element of care, and the role the patient can play in helping achieve the expected outcomes are discussed.

The potential benefits of the patient conference underscore its importance. Properly conducted, the conference can:

- Provide realistic expectations about the probable length of stay in the facility, anticipated functional recovery, and typical daily activities.
- Allay any unfounded fears or apprehensions about the patient's condition or stay in the facility.
- Reveal additional insights to the patient care team about the patient's feelings.
- Motivate the patient to actively cooperate with the patient care team in achieving specified goals.
- Resolve any reservations about any aspect of the care plan.

Conferring with the family. There are many occasions when it is necessary or desirable to confer with the patient's family following the planning conference. The family's involvement and support are especially important to the achievement of expected outcomes. It is understood, however, that the family is only involved with the knowledge and consent of the patient. Although circumstances vary, whenever possible the conference is conducted with both the patient and the family present. Family conferences are usually the responsibility of the social worker, but it may be desirable to include other specialists with special involvement in the patient's care. Whoever conducts the conference should plan to discuss these general areas of concern:

40

- The patient's current status, with special emphasis on the particular reasons for admission.
- The patient's prognosis and the outcomes he or she can expect to achieve in resolving existing problems and functional deficiencies.
- The care program that the planning team has designed to help achieve these goals.
- The care team's expectations of the patient and his or her family in order to obtain maximum benefit from the stay in the facility.

While it is neither possible nor desirable to prescribe a universal formula, certain general principles should be kept in mind when preparing for the patient/family conference:

- Except in unusual circumstances, the conference should be scheduled within 24 to 48 hours after the planning conference. Family conferences are usually scheduled to occur within one week and should accommodate the family's schedule.
- While the conference should not arouse unrealistic hopes in either the patient or the family, the general tone should be positive and optimistic.
- The patient's and family's feelings and level of understanding, *not* the staff's should determine what is said and how it is said.
- In discussing what the care team expects from the patient and the family, it is important to be specific and firm.

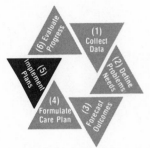

Step 5. Implementing the plan and recording progress. An important part of the problem/ need-oriented patient care system is its systematic method for recording both routine and unusual clinical events in a manner that provides readily accessible feedback on each of the patient's problems/needs. It relies on two types of records: **(1)** *SOAP notes.* SOAP notes differ from traditional narratives notes. They are structured around specific problems/ needs, with each entry numbered and titled to correspond with the need being addressed. They are written only when significant events occur relating to an existing problem/need, when events suggest the development of a new problem/ need, or when government regulations or internal policies dictate.

Problem/need-oriented progress notes also differ from traditional narrative notes in that they follow the SOAP format:

S *Subjective* data are contributed by the patient and the family (e.g., complaints, concerns, reported symptoms, beliefs, attitudes). Subjective information ("soft" data) is never ignored.

O *Objective* data are derived from such sources as physiological tests, laboratory findings, and sensory observations of personnel caring for the patient ("hard" data).

A *Assessment* is the writer's interpretation of subjective and objective data focusing on the nature and origin of an existing or new problem/need. The assessment includes the writer's judgment about the probable outcome.

P *Plan* describes new or altered actions that will be followed to achieve the expected outcome for the problem. This element of the progress note includes plans for information gathering, interventions, and patient/family education.

In addition, each SOAP note includes the date of entry, the problem number and title, the discipline or department

0

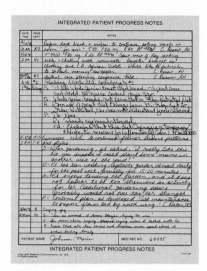

making the entry, and the signature and title or position of the writer.

In addition to SOAP notes, the integrated patient progress notes also include notes which document certain events and isolated facts, such as physician visits, the receipt of drugs, and specimens sent to laboratories. These entries are written in the traditional narrative style.

(2) *Flow sheets.* Repetitive or routine actions and observations are recorded on flow sheets in either tabular or graphic form. The sheets provide a continuous record of objective data for monitoring any specific parameter or for recording discrete events. They also offer a simple and economical means of recording rapidly accumulating data, permitting the care team to monitor the patient's status continuously, easily and chronologically. Use of flow sheets also reduces the need for writing voluminous narrative notes.

Flow sheets may be a simple grid or be specially designed for a given purpose. Specialized flow sheets include those used for documenting fluid input and output, drug administration, and retraining programs.

CHAPTER 4: Patient Evaluation and Quality Assurance: Step 6. Reviewing and Revising Care Plans

The growing importance of quality assurance as a public policy issue has led to nearly universal agreement that in the near future some system of patient evaluation and quality assessment will be mandatory in LTCF's. It is crucial that providers help shape a valid and workable system to insure that it squares with the unique realities, needs, and resources of LTCF's. It goes without saying that the system must focus on the outcomes of care rather than merely its structural elements or the processes by which care is delivered. While structure (i.e., buildings, services, and trained personnel) and process (e.g., individual care plans, established policies and procedures) are important, the ultimate question is whether the patient is progressing as expected toward realistic goals or outcomes given his or her particular set of problems/needs.

In acute-care hospitals, outcome assessment hinges on the patient's status at discharge. The logical question is whether providers produced the "cure" they intended and the patient expected. In long-term care, quality assessment is much less straightforward because of the many important differences between the two settings, differences that must be taken into account when evaluating care:

- Unlike acute-care patients, the focus of care for long-term patients is their multiple medical, functional, and psychosocial problems/needs. Thus, evaluation must address the outcomes of numerous interrelated interventions.

- Unlike acute-care patients, many long-term patients are never discharged and others leave after stays lasting months or years. Hence, evaluation cannot focus on relatively simple short-term outcomes; quality must be evaluated in terms of both long-range goals and shorter-term outcomes staged for assessment at selected periods of time.

- LTCF's must be more concerned than hospitals with quality of life, as they strive over extended periods of time to restore or maintain health and functional capacity while also fulfilling social, emotional, and leisure needs. This requires special therapies and an interdisciplinary effort in assessing patients' needs and strengths, planning and providing care, and evaluating outcomes.

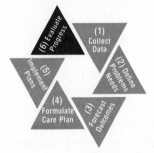

The problem/need-oriented system, which comes to terms with the realities of long-term care, offers LTCF's proved tools and procedures for assuring quality care. A key element is periodic care plan review and revision (step 6) in which the patient's progress toward clearly defined and measurable goals or expected outcomes is analyzed by the care team. The analysis triggers a reevaluation of the patient's problems/needs, which in turn reactivates the entire cycle.

Patient evaluation is incorporated into the problem/need-oriented system by means of scheduled quarterly team reviews and monthly reviews by specific disciplines or specialists. The success of the system lies in developing a day-by-day attitude of reflection and evaluation by all care team members. Patient evaluation should *not* be regarded solely as a periodic exercise but rather as an ongoing process.

Quarterly Team Reviews

The basic vehicle for patient evaluation is the quarterly team review, an interdisciplinary process in which every team member participates in evaluating a selected group of patients. (The number of patients reviewed will depend on the size of the facility and the experience and efficiency of the review team.) The process involves a comprehensive analysis of each patient's progress in achieving or failing to achieve expected outcomes. Revisions are then made in the patient care plan and communicated to appropriate persons. Although the team also reviews the patient's chart for currency, accuracy, and completeness, this is an incidental concern since it is an ongoing function of the various specialists who review the charts monthly.

Analyzing the patient's progress toward expected outcomes involves three basic steps:

(1) Has the patient achieved the stated goal? This is usually a relatively simple judgment based on data available in flow sheets and charted progress notes and the team's first hand knowledge. Remember, expected outcomes always include specific measurable parameters, such as laboratory values, observable behavior, or functional abilities. If the expected outcome has been achieved, that fact is recorded in a progress note and a new goal along with a plan for achieving that goal is written. If the goal has not been achieved, the team analyzes the reasons for nonachievement.

(2) Analyzing the reasons for nonachievement. The reasons may be obvious but more often than not are obscure. Sometimes, more than one reason is involved. The analysis may require careful scrutiny of the patient's record. The JCAH's Quality Resource Center and its Council for Long-Term Care Facilities have written some valuable guidelines designed to aid the search for reasons for nonachievement.* Those guidelines are:

- Was the goal set for the patient reasonable and appropriate?
- Were the approaches, treatments, procedures, and medications appropriate for achieving the intended goal?
- Were the appropriate people designated to carry out the care plan? Did they clearly understand their responsibility, and were they adequately supervised? Did they, in fact, carry out the care plan properly and consistently?
- Were the proper equipment, personnel, and other resources available to properly carry out the care plan?

---

* Imbiorski, W. J., et. al. "The new long term care evaluation procedure—Part 1." **Quality Review Bulletin**, July, 1976, pp. 5–31.

- Did an intervening diagnosis or complication prevent goal achievement?
- Did unforeseen circumstances that prevented goal achievement occur (e.g., the death of a relative, changing the patient's room or roommate, an accident)?

(3) **Taking corrective action.** If nonachievement is caused by unforeseen circumstances or the development of medical problems or complications beyond the control of the care team, corrective action may not be possible. More often, however, analysis will reveal remediable reasons for nonachievement. In either case, a SOAP note is written summarizing the team's conclusions about why the goal has not been achieved and outlining the corrective actions to be taken. In general, corrective actions fall into these categories:

(A) *Reevaluating and redefining the expected outcome.* Failure to achieve an expected outcome may indicate that the patient's problem/need is more severe than realized or that other problems are retarding progress. Or, the goal may have been appropriate but the stated time frame may have been unrealistic. In either case, a redefinition of the expected outcome is in order, perhaps using intermediate goals leading in stages to a longer-term outcome.

(B) *Reevaluating the interventive approaches and procedures and formulating an alternative care plan to achieve the desired outcome.* The goal may have been realistic, but the planned interventions may not be effective. An alternative care plan is called for based on the team's assessment of the patient, her or his total situation, and the resources available.

(C) *Restructuring the manner in which the care plan is implemented.* The goal may be realistic and the planned interventions appropriate, but some breakdown may have occurred in implementing the plan. Perhaps the wrong personnel were designated. Or, there may have been a failure to communicate clearly with those expected to implement the plan. Perhaps they lacked the necessary skills or background information to understand and carry out their responsibilities. Or, the failure may have been due to negligence or lack of time. Whatever the reason, corrective action may lie in designating someone else to implement the plan or in making sure that the responsible person understands and does his or her duty.

(D) *Obtaining the necessary resources to implement the plan properly.* Nonachievement may have resulted from a lack of proper equipment or specialized personnel or insufficient staff time to implement the plan properly. While corrective actions may be apparent, resolving the problem may or may not be possible. In any case, a report and recommendation to management are probably indicated.

In addition to scheduled quarterly team reviews, patient evaluation is often triggered by unscheduled events and circumstances that are familiar everyday occurrences in LTCF's. These "natural" review occasions call for intervention planning that cannot be postponed until the next scheduled team review. While it may be possible and even desirable to confer with colleagues, unscheduled, or impromptu, reviews can and should be performed promptly by appropriate individual team members. Some common occasions for reviewing all or part of a patient's care plan are:

- A marked change in one or more of the patient's identified problems.
- The development of a new problem or need.
- The patient's failure to respond to interventions.
- The occurrence of a specified target date for achieving a specific restorative goal.
- A mandated (either by regulation or the facility's internal policies) schedule of progress note writing.

■ Information generated by special diagnostic workups.

The nature and extent of these unscheduled reviews will vary, depending on the precipitating event. However, the review process always involves the step-by-step problem-solving sequence outlined in chapter 3. For example, impromptu reviews are always triggered by significant new information. The new information might be based on laboratory tests or other special diagnostic workups, or it could derive from the reviewer's survey of charted progress notes and flow sheets or from personal clinical observations or judgments about the patient's progress toward stated goals. Whatever the case, the reviewer is in possession of important new data (step 1) that must be assessed in the context of the patient's total situation. The review may mean defining a problem/need hitherto unrecognized or redefining (or retitling) an existing problem (step 2). New or redefined problems then require the formulation of appropriate expected outcomes (step 3) and the development of new or revised care plans (step 4). The plan is then recorded in the patient's record and communicated to all members of the care team. The plan is put into action (step 5) and scheduled for future review and possible revision (step 6).

In the problem/need-oriented system, patient evaluation can be a superb learning experience for the care team. Writing challenging but realistic expected outcomes is more an art than a science. Patients differ widely, of course, and respond to the same therapeutic approaches at varying rates, even when those approaches are appropriate and consistently executed. Thus, even the outcomes expected by experienced patient care teams are only "best estimates" of the progress a given patient is capable of making.

The object is not to be correct in every case but to make a conscientious attempt to establish realistic, challenging expectations that are measurable. Care teams that are always "on target" in achieving patient goals or that consistently fall short of those targets are both suspect. The expectations of the former are probably not challenging enough, while those of the latter are unrealistic or else the team is learning nothing from its analysis of the reasons for nonachievement. Goals will sometimes be reached and sometimes they will not be. If not, the analysis of why an expected outcome has not been achieved will always be revealing and can lead to new insights and corrective actions that will improve the quality of care throughout the facility.

Monthly Reviews by Specific Disciplines

The care plan review process also calls for monthly reviews by individual disciplines represented on the care team. This procedure keeps each specialist in close touch with the total clinical picture for each patient for whom he or she has special responsibility, assures the accuracy and currency of charted information relevant to each discipline, and fulfills federal and state regulations. Monthly reviews by discipline focus on those patients and specific problems for which each specialist has responsibility. In addition to reviewing, evaluating, and revising relevant care plans, each specialist analyzes the achievement of restorative goals whose evaluation dates coincide with the monthly review.

When carrying out the monthly review, it is useful to observe written guidelines or protocols such as these:

General Guidelines: Monthly Care Plan Review

(1) Is the problem/need list complete and current, and has the visible file been updated?

- Add new problems
- Retitle old problems
- Transfer problems from active to inactive column

(2) Are expected outcomes in order?

- Have they been achieved?
- Are they still appropriate (i.e., challenging but realistic)?
- Are time frames (i.e., evaluation dates) for restorative goals realistic?

(3) Are care plans (i.e., Dx, Rx. and Ed) in order?

- Do they reflect current interventions?
- Are they appropriate for achieving stated goals?
- Is accountability designated?

(4) Are rehabilitation potential and discharge plans updated to reflect the patient's current status?

Because the specific concerns of the specialties vary, each specialist should conduct the monthly review according to her or his own written protocols, which may be adapted from the preceding general guidelines. An example of the monthly review protocols used by dietary services follows:

Review Protocols/Monthly Care Plan Review: Dietary Services

(1) Verify the accuracy of dietary orders in the health record and correlate with dietary services' visible file.

- Check against information on transfer and clinic referral forms.
- Check against latest written or telephone orders from the physician.

(2) Review flow sheets for weight and urine sugar values.

- Review for weight changes (unless intended) that exceed these ranges:
  ± 4 lbs. during the past 30 days.
  ±10 lbs. during the past six months.
- Review for urine sugar values as follows:
  Urine sugar values consistently 4+.
  Spillage patterns by time of day.
  If on insulin, urine sugar values that are consistently negative.

(3) Review current laboratory reports on fasting blood sugar and hemoglobin for abnormal values.

NOTE: If abnormalities are found in protocol 2 or 3, then—
(a) Discuss with consulting dietitian
(b) Add new problem to problem/need list.
(c) Write SOAP note, emphasizing care plan.
(d) Add to master care plan and visible file care plan.

(4) Review problem/need list for completeness.

- Add new problems that are identified.
- Write SOAP note.

(5) Evaluate the need for continuing present texture changes.

- *GOAL:* less severe modification whenever possible.

(6) Review progress notes written during the past 30 days, noting dietary problems observed by others that have not been communicated to you.

(7) Check care plan for goals scheduled for evaluation that are your responsibility.

- Was the goal achieved?
- Analyze reasons for nonachievement.
- Write SOAP note, emphasizing changes and correctable actions, based on your analysis.
- Enter changes in care plan and communicate with team leader.

(8) If significant changes are identified, discuss with team leader for possible revision conference.

As one expert in patient evaluation has pointed out, "Quality review mechanisms are effective only to the extent that there is a commitment to make them work. A relatively crude procedure, seriously applied, is probably more effective than a highly sophisticated technique to which only lip service is given." We believe the problem/need-oriented system includes a sound, workable process for evaluating patients and assuring quality care. Yet, the process is only as good as the efforts invested in making it work. For those who are serious in their quest for quality, there is no better system.

CHAPTER 5: Maintaining and Improving the Problem/Need-Oriented System

The benefits of problem/need-oriented patient care for both patients and staff are substantial and will soon become apparent. As they do, they will tend to reward and sustain the interests and efforts of those involved in the program. Yet, like most worthwhile things, this program needs cultivation if it is to grow and thrive.

Avoiding Common Pitfalls

One way to sustain interest in, and improve, the problem/need-oriented patient care process is to be aware of and correct any weakness in the process. In the table below, a number of common pitfalls are listed together with comments to assist you in dealing with them. The pitfalls deal with shortcomings in administration, group process, and methodology.

Pitfalls	Comments
ADMINISTRATIVE	
■ Failing to set a definite time and place for patient care planning conferences.	■ Find the "best time and place"; then regard it as sacred.
■ Neglecting to notify team members about the patient agenda far enough in advance to permit adequate preparation.	■ *RULE:* five to seven days advance notice. *Suggestion:* give each team member a set of preparation worksheets filled in with names of patients to be conferenced.
■ Carelessness about starting conferences on time.	■ Be businesslike about starting on time; deal with tardiness promptly and firmly.
■ Allowing unnecessary interruptions.	■ *RULE:* allow only emergency phone calls and interruptions.
■ Failing to rotate team leadership at appropriate intervals.	■ *Suggestion:* Rotate position every three to six months, in order to: keep the group fresh, spread the work, and build a corps of trained leaders.

Pitfalls	Comments
■ Not having appropriate policies and procedures for resolving administrative or performance problems.	■ For example: — If one or two team members can't attend, should the conference be postponed? What constitutes a quorum? Who makes these decisions? — If a team member hasn't prepared, should anything be done or said? Who's responsible?

GROUP PROCESS

■ Holding conferences in rooms that are not conducive to serious and productive discussion.	■ Minimize distractions such as rooms that are too small, too cold, too hot, too stuffy, or too noisy.
■ Tolerating a lack of advance preparation by team members.	■ The greatest single deterrent to effective care planning! *Suggestion:* try collecting preparation worksheets with signatures from each team member as a preventive measure!
■ Prolonging conferences unduly.	■ *Suggestion:* Schedule as many patients as can be comfortably discussed in 60 to 90 minutes. (Quarterly review meetings may last longer.) Longer meetings are counterproductive; restlessness increases and productivity falls.
■ Allowing the group process to break down usually because the team leader or some other strong personality dominates, preventing true interaction.	■ Anything that hinders open interaction among team members should be promptly identified and resolved.
■ Failing to draw timid team members (e.g., nursing assistants) into the team discussion.	■ Lack of full participation limits the effectiveness of patient care planning and delivery.
■ Straying from the subject.	■ Brief "asides" are often useful; repeated and/or extended straying is symptomatic of some unresolved problem or problems on this list.

Pitfalls	Comments
■ Not using a chalkboard or over-head projector.	■ Use of these aids focuses the team's attention and holds important points before them.
■ Using team conferences as occasions for staff development programs.	■ Conferences (especially quarterly reviews) frequently uncover gaps in knowledge that should be followed up by inservice educational programs. *RULE:* The conference itself must *never* be used for informal lectures or formal educational presentations.

METHODOLOGICAL

■ Making common errors in preparing the written health care plan.	■ *RULES:* — Master Problem/Need List, Master Health Care Plan, & Visible Record Health Plan must be completed *during* the conference by designated scribes. — Print or write legibly; typing and rewriting later wastes time. — The team leader is *never* responsible for completing the written forms.
■ Falling victim to the "Merck Manual Syndrome" (i.e., compulsive reporting of every detail of the patient's medical and social history, and delving into esoteric aspects of his current condition) in collecting and reporting the data base.	■ *RULE:* Limit data collection and reporting to information that is relevant to the patient's current problems/needs and to the development of an effective care plan.
■ Reading, instead of summarizing the relevant highlights of the patient data base (i.e., histories and assessments).	■ Team members should be aware of what others have said and should limit their contributions to new information relevant to care planning.

Pitfalls	Comments
■ Limiting the problem/need list to diagnosed physical problems.	■ *RULE:* In addition to physical and functional problems/needs, systematically identify: routine health maintenance needs; social, behavioral, or leisure-related problems; and lifestyle preferences.
■ Laboring over the titles of problems/needs as though your professional reputation is on the line!	■ *RULE:* All problems/needs must be defined in terms of the team's present level of knowledge and understanding.
■ Writing expected outcome statements *after* the care plan has been developed.	■ Remember, expected outcomes are meant to shape care plans!
■ Limiting expected outcome statements to problems/needs where the goal is restoration.	■ *RULE:* Expected outcome statements must be written for *every* problem/need, including those where prevention, maintenance, or palliation is the objective.
■ Failing to include the basic elements of a good expected outcome statement.	
■ Failing to communicate the care plan (or care plan revisions) to the appropriate persons following the conference.	■ *RULE:* Care plans (and revisions) must be communicated to all personnel involved in caring for the patient. *Suggestion:* Post a list of patients with new or revised care plans at the appropriate nursing station, asking staff to review these plans.

Improving Performance

At its best, the problem/need-oriented patient care process is a highly skilled, but masterable, art. Mastery depends in part on experience and in part on the deliberate efforts of program leaders to improve the proficiency of the team and its individual members. Two major areas of concern are (1) the techniques of patient assessment and care plan design, and **(2)** the skill of participation in the interdisciplinary team process.

The ability to perceive and assess each patient's unique needs and strengths, and to create care programs that optimize the patient's physical and social well-being involves knowledge and skills that can be taught and nurtured. Those responsible for the program should work with the staff development coordinator to develop special programs to help team members acquire:

- The ability to establish relationships of trust that encourage open communication with patients and their families.
- The ability to synthesize facts, and one's own insights and expertise, in order to understand the patient and to plan effectively for his care.
- The ability to search out available resources and to use them creatively in working out programs of patient care.

A smooth-functioning, productive interdisciplinary planning team is characterized by open communication. Although this rarely happens automatically, the skills of conducting and participating in such a group can be learned.

Since the effectiveness of the group process depends largely on skilled leadership, team leaders must understand the dynamics of the group process. They should know how interpersonal conflicts develop and manifest themselves, how they can be resolved, and how the efforts of specialists can be yoked into productive team practice. Although such a discussion is beyond this manual's scope, it is suggested that team leaders:

- Read all they can about team building, group process, and group leadership.
- Take advantage of classes and seminars on these subjects.
- Invite an expert on team building and group process to a meeting of the planning team to offer criticisms and suggestions.

Team members also can be helped to improve their group skills. It is recommended that team leaders:

- Work with the staff development coordinator to plan special training opportunities in team participation and group process.
- Using the "instant replay" technique, periodically ask team members to express their feelings about how a particular meeting went, what went wrong (or right) and why, and what can be done to improve the group process.
- Consider using an evaluation checklist, like the one in appendix 3, to periodically assess the team's performance.

Building and Sustaining Interest

It is important to work at building and sustaining the care team's interest in the problem/need-oriented system. Involvement and recognition are two time-tested ways to do so. Below are a few general suggestions on how to keep care team members involved and how to recognize and reward their efforts. Hopefully, these suggestions will trigger your own ideas about how to build and maintain staff interest.

Since personal involvement increases interest, the team leader should make a special effort to:

- Patiently encourage hesitant, nonparticipating team members to express their insights and ideas about patients.
- Utilize the interests and abilities of individual team members by occasionally asking them to report briefly on special patient needs or new services. Pass the assignments around.

Remember, one good way to build and hold staff interest is by recognizing and rewarding the care team's efforts. Here are a few simple but proved techniques:

- Spend a few minutes at the start of the team conference passing out verbal rewards, such as comments by patients (or their families) about their care, especially when that care reflects favorably on the team's planning efforts.

- During the planning conference, remember to acknowledge and praise particularly useful contributions from individual members.

- Publicize the new problem/need-oriented patient care program. This will cultivate pride and enhance esprit de corps. Some ideas are: **(1)** write an article about the program for publication in your association's magazine or newsletter; **(2)** ask a local newspaper to do a human interest story on some unique aspect of the program; **(3)** prepare a presentation about the program for the next meeting of your association or professional colleagues. The planning team could actually "demonstrate" the planning process using a fictitious patient; or **(4)** invite leaders from other long-term care facilities to your planning conference meetings and volunteer to help them start such a program.

Epilogue

In the prologue we said that this book is intended to be a "how to" manual with enough detail to enable the reader to use it in implementing the problem/need-oriented system. We hope we have kept faith with that promise and that the book is already beginning to work for you.

We add two final words of caution. The first is that, while the problem/need-oriented system is a superb patient management tool ideally suited for long-term care, it is *only* a tool. In the hands of caring practitioners searching for ways to enhance their craft, the problem/need-oriented system offers tools that will not disappoint. Results will come in direct proportion to how well those tools are used. Those who are looking for labor-saving gadgets, however, will find no magic here—or anywhere else!

Our second word of caution is that the manual is not intended to answer every question or fit every circumstance as you begin to implement the problem/need-oriented system. Obviously, flexibility is necessary as you apply the system's principles to the unique needs and resources of your facility. Encouragingly, during the past decade these principles have proved flexible enough to fit the needs of a vast array of health care settings—medical schools, hospitals, doctors'offices and clinics, and nursing homes. They have worked for us, and we are convinced they will work for you too.

Glossary

Active Problem/Need: Any problem, need or life-style preference (except "acute self-limiting problems") that currently concern the patient and/or those planning and providing for his care.

Acute Self-Limiting Problem: A temporary (less than 10 days' duration) problem that is self-limiting (e.g., head cold, "crying jag"). Listed separately from the Master Problem/Need List to avoid making that list too unwieldly.

Conference Coordinator: Works with the Conference Team Leader to arrange all patient care planning conferences and quarterly team review meetings.

Conference Team Leader: Plans and leads patient care planning conferences and quarterly team review meetings. Selected primarily for leadership ability, the Team Leader can be any competent health professional.

Data Base: Information collected and recorded about a patient and obtained by examination, observation, personal interview or judgments. The *initial data base*, gathered at the time of admission, includes both historic and assessment information. Types of data base information include: laboratory test results, physical examination findings, histories, observations and assessments.

Expected Outcome: A judgment by the planning conference team about the probable result of an optimal care plan for a particular problem or need. Includes goals which connote restoration of health or function, but more frequently in long term care the emphasis is on outcomes involving the maintenance of existing health or functional levels, and the prevention or palliation of illness. Expected outcomes are determined for each active problem or need, and provide the focus for planning and evaluating care.

Flow Sheet: Used to record routine or repetitive actions or observations in either graphic or tabular form, and allows practitioners to evaluate trends in such information. It may supplement information contained in progress notes.

Inactive Problem/Need: An active problem/need that has been resolved either by intervention or by natural processes. The
resolved problem/need is transferred to the inactive
problem/need column, along with the date of resolution.

Initial Assessment of Rehabilitation Potential: Formulated at the initial planning conference a formal assessment statement rep-
resenting the planning team's best judgment (i.e., prognosis) about the functioning level the patient can probably
attain or maintain with optimal rehabilitative intervention.
Includes reasons supporting this judgment. This statement
expresses the intended outcome of the overall program of
care planned for the patient, and can be regarded as the
long term goal.

Initial Discharge Plan: Developed at the initial planning conference,
it is the team's prognosis about the probability of the patient's discharge from the long term care facility, and includes the likely destination.

Integrated Care Plan: A program of care developed by the planning
conference team for active problems/needs. A separate care
plan is developed to achieve expected outcomes stated for
each problem, which includes one or more of the following
elements:

> **Dx:** Plans for gathering additional information to define or
> clarify a problem, or to monitor the patient's progress.
> **Rx:** Interventions planned to achieve expected outcomes.
> **Ed:** Plans for informing and/or instructing patients/families
> about a problem or care plan to assure their positive
> involvement.

Interdisciplinary: The interaction of two or more disciplines or
specialists, in pooling their expertise to work toward common objectives. Contrast with *multi*disciplinary which
merely connotes the involvement of two or more disciplines
in a common endeavor.

Life-Style Preferences: Those unique and individual patient desires, either expressed or demonstrated, which have enhanced or enriched the patient's life, and will continue to support optimal physical and psychosocial health. Their fulfillment is gratifying in and of itself.

Master Health Care Plan: Embodies all of the care plan developed by the planning conference team on a special form, which includes the following elements: problem/need list, expected outcomes, care plan elements and accountability, assessment of rehabilitation potential and initial discharge plan.

Master Problem/Need List: A numbered list of all problems, needs and life-style preferences (except "acute self-limiting problems") that concern the patient and/or those planning and providing for his care. Includes any area of concern in which the patient wants or requires help in attaining or maintaining an optimal level of physical, social, emotional and spiritual function. The list provides the organizational basis and index for the patient's entire health record. (See also "acute self-limiting problems", "primary health needs", "life-style preferences").

Monthly Review of Care Plan by Discipline: A review procedure carried out monthly by each care team discipline of those patients' care plan elements for which they have specific accountability. Review includes analysis of any goals or expected outcomes scheduled for their review at that time, but major emphasis is on the accuracy, currency and appropriateness of relevant care plan elements.

Objective Data: Observable information ("hard data") about a patient from tests, procedures, examinations, and sensory observations collected by a staff member.

Occupational (Departmental) Team: Workers in a single departmental or occupational group within the long term care facility who function as a team in carrying out their daily responsibilities. Occupational teams are linked to one another by their representatives on the interdisciplinary planning conference and patient care teams. (See also "Patient Care Team" and "Planning Conference Team").

Patient Care Planning Conference: A regularly scheduled meeting of the planning conference team in which a selected group of newly admitted patients is systematically reviewed. Each patient's problems and needs are identified, and a comprehensive program of care is designed to achieve realistic goals and expected outcomes established for each problem or need.

Patient Care Team: Representatives from various departmental or occupational groups directly involved in carrying out the patient care plan. An interdisciplinary group coordinating their efforts toward common goals. (See also "Occupational (Department) Team" and "Planning Conference Team").

Planning Conference Team: An interdisciplinary group of staff members who pool their expertise to assess patient problems/ needs and to plan interventions to achieve expected outcomes during patient care planning conferences and quarterly review meetings. (See also "Patient Care Team" and "Occupational Team"). Participants can include:

Director of Nursing and/or Charge Nurse	Therapeutic Recreation Coordinator
Nurses Assistant(s)	Occupational Therapist
Dietitian or D.S.S.	Physical Therapist
Housekeeping Supervisor	Social Worker
Other Specialists such as the Physician, Psychologist, Speech Therapist, Volunteer Coordinator & Clergyman	

Primary Health Needs: Preventive (diagnostic and prophylactic) measures such as periodic pap smears or immunizations planned to avert the development of health problems. A mandatory concern with patients in long term care facilities, whose length of stay often extends for weeks, months or even years. Usually included on the Master Problem/Need List.

Quarterly Team Review of Care Plan: A meeting of the planning conference team in which team members assess the progress of a selected group of patients toward previously established goals or expected outcomes. Analysis of achievement or non-achievement can result in revisions of the expected outcomes and care plans, or in corrective actions designed to properly implement existing plans. Every patient is reviewed at least quarterly, although special circumstances can dictate review at any time.

SOAP Notes: A structured progress note numbered and titled to correspond with the specific problem/need it addresses. Derives its name from its four distinctive elements: (S) subjective data, (O) objective data, (A) the writer's assessment of the data, and (P) his plan for addressing the problem. In the problem-oriented system, SOAP notes replace most traditional narrative notes. (See also "Flow sheets," "Subjective Data," "Objective Data.")

Subjective Data: Information about the patient contributed by the patient or his family. Includes complaints, concerns, reported symptoms and other "soft data."

Visible File Health Care Plan: A convenient desk-top penciled version of the current care plan. It is designed as a "working tool" for all care team personnel and is used in visible file format. It is *not* a legal record.

Appendix 1

Sample Health Record

NOTE: this is an *incomplete* health record. Physician order sheets, medication administration forms, and other information not necessary in the demonstration of the problem/need-oriented system have been omitted.

I.

PATIENT TRANSFER FORM

Name **Johnson** (Last) **Marie** (First) **A.** (M.I.)

Birth Date **5-9-1908** Sex F S.M ⓦ D. Religion **Lutheran**

Home Address **1545 St. Paul Avenue** Zip Code **55116**

Directions _____

Floor **1st** Apt. **108** Tel. **631-7235**

Responsible Relative or Guardian **Mrs. Carol Anderson** **Daughter**

Address **Prior Lake, Minnesota** Tel. **447-7658**

Physician in Charge After Transfer **Mark Welbeing, M.D.** Address **2110 Central Medical Bldg.** Zip Code **55108**

Medical Record No. **78-8-0056** (Referring institution or agency)

Transferred From **Midway Hospital** Station or Clinic **1 South**

Address **1700 University Avenue** Zip Code **55108**

Date of Admission **8-6-1978** Date of this Transfer **8-11-1978**

Transferred to **Gold Medallion Nursing Center** (Name of Hosp., Nursing Home, Agency)

Address **5001 W. 80th Street** Zip Code **55437**

Health Insurance Claim No. **471-62-7346 A**

II. Advised of transfer and consent given by **Mrs. Carol Anderson** (Name) **Daughter** (Relation) Date **8-10-1978**

III.

(Check, explain) Impairments	
Disabilities	Mentality ___
Amputation ___	Speech ___
Paresis ___	Hearing ___
Contracture ___	Vision **X**
Decub. Ulcer ___	Sensation ___

Incontinence

Bowel ___ Bladder ___

Activity Tolerance Limitations
None ___ Moderate **X** Severe ___

ORDERS FOR ACTIVE CARE

BED
Position in good body alignment and change position every_____ hrs.
Avoid _____ position.
Prone position _____ times/day as tolerated.

SIT IN CHAIR ___ hrs. ___ times/day
Increase as tolerated **X**

SELF CARE
Maintain ___ Improve **X** Level.
Interpret progress to family **X**

WEIGHT BEARING
Full **X** Partial ___ None ___
in **both** leg.

LOCOMOTION
Walk **ad lib** times/day
Increase as tolerated

EXERCISES
Range of Motion _____ times/day
to _____
by patient ___ nurse ___ family ___
Other as outlined or attached ___
Stand ___ Min. _____ times/day

SOCIAL ACTIVITIES
Encourage group **X** Individual ___
within ___ outside **X** home.

Transport: Ambulance ___ Car **X**
Car for handicapped ___ Bus ___

I certify that the continuing care herein ordered meets Medicare certification requirements ☑

Patient knows diagnosis? **Yes** Last Chest X-ray Date **8-8-1978**

Attachments: Diet List **X** Lab. Report **X** Exercise Program ___ X-ray Report **X**
(Give Dates) IMPORTANT MEDICAL HISTORY AND PROGNOSIS (State allergies if any)

Prognosis excellent for discharge to less supervised living. No allergies or reactions to medications, insects, food, animals or seasons. Nephrectomy from auto accident 1966. Diverticulitis in 1973.

☐ Employment related. MAJOR DIAGNOSES. Last physical exam. date **8-7-1978**
- Diverticulitis, with rectal bleeding and blood loss anemia.
- Anxiety, secondary to diverticulitis.
- Hypertension. - Obesity. - Constipation. - Osteoarthritis.

PHYSICIAN'S ORDERS (Drugs, diet, supplies, appliances, home health aide, etc.)
1. Achromycin(O), 250mg, qid x 21 days, 2 hrs. a.c. meals.
2. Feosol Spansule, 1 cap bid x 1 month, with meals.
3. Bacimycin ointment/apply to rectal area following bm's and h.s. Wash skin with mild soap before each application.
4. Multivitamin with trace minerals, 1 cap in a.m.
5. Valium, 10 mg, bid PRN for anxiety.
6. Esidrix tabs, 50 mg, 1 tab bid.
7. 1200 calorie, fiber restricted, 3-5gm Na diet.
8. B.P. daily in a.m./call M.D. if B.P. exceeds 180/100.
9. Hemoglobin q month.
10. Weight reduction to 140 lbs.
11. Observe stool for blood.
12. Observe ankle edema/call M.D. if > 2+
13. Elevate feet, 30 min. a.m. & afternoon for ankle edema/PRN.
14. Stool guaiac x 3 consecutive bm's.
15. Force fluids to 2000 cc's daily.
16. Weigh q Monday before breakfast.
17. Colace 100 mg q day in a.m./PRN.
18. Pap smear in November.
19. Bivalent flu vaccine in October.
20. Serum K+ q mo. x 3, then q 3 mo.
21. ASA 10 gr. PRN.

THERAPY ORDERS: ☐ Physical Therapy ☐ Occ. Therapy ☐ Speech Therapy
☐ RPT or OTR: Assess needs, instruct nurse in active nursing care and revise PRN.
☐ RPT or OTR: Assess needs, instruct Activity Dir. in supportive care, revise PRN.
Goals or Objectives:

Physician's Signature *M Welbeing MD* Date **8-11-1978**

Developed by Minneapolis Health Dept. 1963. Revised 1964, 1966 and 1969.

72

IV. PATIENT INFORMATION

SELF CARE STATUS

Check level of performance. Use S in column for supervision only. Draw line when item is currently inapplicable.

In blank space explain assistance needed in care. Use number from table to identify area discussed. Therapists and social workers include title with signature.

	Independent	Needs Assistance	Unable to do	
Bed Activity	X			1. Turns
	X			2. Sits
Personal Hygiene	X			3. Face, Hair, Arms
	X			4. Trunk & Perineum
	X			5. Lower Extremities
	X			6. Bladder Program
	X			7. Bowel Program
Dressing	X			8. Upper Trunk, Arms
	X			9. Lower Trunk, Legs
				10. Appliance, Splint
Transfer	X			11. Feeding
	X			12. Sitting
	X			13. Standing
	X			14. Tub
	X			15. Toilet
Loco-motion				16. Wheelchair
	X			17. Walking
	X			18. Stairs

19. PERSONAL INTERESTS   Music X
    Group Singing X   Group Games____
    Crafts____   Radio and TV X   Art____
    Plays Instrument X   Other X

20. MENTAL STATUS   Lonely____
    Alert X   Forgetful____   Confused____
    Other____

21. COMMUNICATIONS ABILITY   (Yes, No)
    Speaks and Understands   Yes
    Writes Intelligibly   Yes
    Understands Writing   Yes
    (If No or any limitations, describe)
    Responds to Gestures (describe)   ____

22. OTHER NURSING INFORMATION
    about diagnosis, medications, treatments, medical history, habits, preferences, condition on discharge, etc.

23. EQUIPMENT
    Side Rails Bedboard____ Footboard____
    Long: R____ L____   Short: R____ L____

24. BED: Low X   Mattress: Firm X Reg.____
    Other____

Mrs. Johnson is alert and performs ADLs independently. She ambulates well but complains of being "stiff" in knees in morning. She has no complaints of pain re: her diverticulitis, but is very anxious about the rectal bleeding. She feels that she has cancer and that "no one is telling her the truth." Since she is hypertensive, this anxiety can elevate her BP. Because she is obese, she tends to tire easily. She needs instruction with her diet. Her last BM was 8/10/78, and her last meal was lunch. Her appetite is excellent, and she sleeps well without a sedative but gets up to go the B.R. during the night. There is some "blurring" of vision.

Nurse's Sig. _Dorothy Johnson R.N._   Tel. 636-2340   Ext. 42

V. SOCIAL INFORMATION
(Adjustment to disability, emotional support from family, motivation for self care, socializing ability, financial plan, family health problem, etc.) (Chief previous occupations.)

Agencies Active____   Sig.____

IDENTIFYING DATA: 70 year old white, ambulatory female who is a reliable historian.

CHIEF CONCERN: Blood in the stool.

HPI: Appearance of small amount of bright red blood in stools approximately 2 weeks ago. Bleeding has since occurred intermittently and in varying amounts. Stool has been darker in color than usual and blood tinged. A long history of constipation has been more severe without any bouts of diarrhea. Relates two recent episodes of acute pain in left lower quadrant which subsided after a few days. Denies nausea/vomiting. Perianal irritation occurred following several hours of rectal bleeding and skin is now reportedly "raw." An eight year history of diverticulosis accompanies this woman.

PMH:
| Tonsillectomy | -- | Childhood | St. Mary's Hospital |
| Appendectomy | | | |

Nephrectomy	--	1966	County Medical Center
Pneumonia	--	1970	St. Mary's Hospital
Diverticulosis	--	1970	Outpatient
Hypertension	--	1975	Outpatient

Denies any drug or food allergies.

Current medication: Esidrix 25 mg ī BID
Colace 100 mg q.d. am PRN

Immunization -- Tetanus toxoid, 1970.

PATIENT PROFILE: Widowed x 6 years; living alone in senior citizen high rise. Sustains many interests in various club activities, but recently has curtailed outside events due to abdominal discomforts. Gets no routine exercise. Enjoys reading, but notes problems with blurring vision. Son (M.D.) and daughter (P.T.) live locally and are in frequent contact with patient. Eats regular diet with 3-4 cups coffee/day. No alcohol or cigarettes.

ROS: Generally tires easily. Has gradually been gaining weight. Denies skin or hair changes other than perianal breakdown. Hearing functional. Eyes blurring x 6 mos. without pain. Wears glasses. Denies cough, dyspnea, chest pain, palpitations, or leg cramps. Mild bilateral ankle swelling present for many years. G.I. system as described in HPI. No upper G.I. distress. No problems with genital-urinary tract. Has occasional aching of hands, shoulders, and knees without redness or swelling. Denies headaches, dizziness, limb weakness, or loss of balance. Relates anxiety over cancer since time of husband's death from lung cancer. No signs of depression; normal sleep pattern.

HISTORY AND PHYSICAL

FORM H-2A (5-77)

PHYSICAL EXAMINATION: Vital Signs: Wt. 169   Ht. 5'3"   BP 180/96   T. 99   P. 84

General Appearance: Pale, elderly female in moderate degree of physical distress and mental anxiety. Obese; neatly groomed.

Skin & Hair: Contiguous erythematous, weeping excoriation of perianal area extending onto buttock. Approximately 7 cm in diameter. Senile keratoses of neck and shoulders.

HEENT: Normocephalic. Ears neg. with functional hearing. Neg. nose and throat. Edentulous with proper fitting dentures. PERRLA. Intact EOMs and visual fields. Central clouding of lens bilaterally. Fundi poorly visualized without dilitation.

Lymphatics: Negative.

Neck: Trachea midline. Thyroid non-palpable; no masses. Full ROM.

Thorax/Lungs: Clear to percussion and auscultation.

Heart: Normal sinus rhythm, S_1 and S_2. No S_3 or S_4. Short early grade III/VI systolic murmur at aortic area. No bruits. Peripheral pulses strong and equal.

Breasts: No discharge, discoloration or masses.

Abdomen: Incisional scar left flank. Tenderness to palpation over left quadrants with more acute pain in LLQ. Palpable descending large bowel. Liver and spleen neg.

Genitalia: External and pelvic exam nl. for age.

Rectal: Normal sphincter tone. Without masses or significant hemorrhoids. Small amount of desiccated stool palpable.

Back and Extremities: Mild kyphosis without bony or muscle tenderness. Mild leg varicosities bilaterally. 1+ edema both ankles. Arthritic changes of finger and knee joints; without measurable functional deficit.

Neuro: Cranial nerves 11-X11 WNL. DTRs physiologic. Balance and Gait WNL.

Emotional: Stable history; intact intellectual functions of orientation and cognition. Slight impairment of recent memory. No depression, but highly anxious at this time over health.

Summary of Condition/Assessment

Rectal bleeding and perianal skin breakdown. R/O ca colon, diverticulitis, ulcerative colitis.

75

DISCHARGE SUMMARY:

Mrs. Johnson, a 70 year old caucasian widow is being discharged for nursing
home convalescence following a 6-day hospital stay for the primary problem
of diverticulitis. Admission was through the ER on 8/6/1978.

Medical history at time of admission included a diagnosis of diverticulosis
x 8 years, hypertension and a nephrectomy in 1966. There was no allergies.
Medications from home were Esidrix 25 mg BID, and Colace 100 mg $\overline{q}$d PRN.

Admission findings revealed a two week history of intermittent red, rectal
bleeding and left lower quadrant pain accompanied by severe constipation and
excoriation of the perianal skin. Physical examination further demonstrated
obesity and a benign heart murmur. Visual impairment was noted on history
with cataract formation evident upon cursory eye examination. The large
colon was visually assessed with proctoscopy and sigmoidoscopy, which revealed
extensive diverticula of the sigmoid colon with multiple sites of inflamma-
tion and petechial hemorrhage. There was no evidence of mucosal sloughing;
hemorrhoids were inactive. Barium enema demonstrated diverticula formation
throughout the entire colon, particularly at the sigmoid and distal descending
colon regions with evidence of diverticulitis. There was no evidence of
colonic masses.

Admission laboratory studies showed Hgb. of 10.5 and Hct. of 33 vol.% with
normal indices. Chemistry profile, potassium and serum thyroid were WNL.
Blood pressure during hospital stay ranged from 185/110 to 155/95. TPR was
WNL. A high degree of anxiety was present on admission and appeared somewhat
abated at discharge.

The diverticulitis was treated with Achromycin 250 mg qid, and an oral iron
supplement was instituted in response to blood loss anemia. Hgb. at the time
of discharge was 11 gm. Topical treatment of the perianal excoriation with
antibacterial ointment decreased erythema with notable improvement of super-
ficial lesions. The anxiety state was managed moderately well on a trial
of 10 mg Valium BID.

At the time of discharge, the LLQ discomfort was markedly diminished and the
stool guaiac registered 1+. It was mutually determined with Mrs. Johnson
that a period of convalescence would be needed for stabilizing her program
of bowel management and for a general regaining of strength. Arrangements
for transfer to an intermediate level of nursing care were made with an excellent potential for rehabilitation to independent living.

Final diagnoses: Diverticulosis; resolving diverticulitis with secondary
blood loss anemia and perianal skin excoriations; hypertension; visual impairment probably secondary to cataracts; obesity; constipation; anxiety; and osteoarthritis.

NURSING HISTORY

ADMISSION DATE
8-11-78

Biographical

Ambulatory, caucasian 70 yr. female. Reliable historian.

Chief Complaint

#1 Wants to get stronger after hospital stay of one week and go home. Expresses fear and dislike of becoming dependent on children.

#2 Concerned about whether present "bowel" problems will get better. Asks "is it cancer?"

History of Present Illness

See medical history and transfer form for medical history and current meds. Understands reasons for taking all meds presently ordered.

Past History

No known allergies. Weight gain of 20# in last 18 mos. Had been overweight. Immunized in 1970 with Tetanus Toxoid. Denies receiving flu shots.

Patient Profile

Widowed housewife who intends to return to prior living arrangements in senior highrise. Enjoys intellectual activities such as music, literature and poetry. Was involved in social activities connected with Lutheran church, political party, garden club and bridge.

Does not smoke or drink alcohol. Has not modified her diet except for a dislike for vegetables and difficulty drinking more

Signature of person completing form   Date

PATIENT NAME Johnson, Marie   MED REC NO. 68495

NURSING HISTORY

ADMISSION DATE
8-11-78

than a glass or two of water a day. Likes 3-4 cups of coffee in morning to "get started."

Has had weekly beauty shop appointment until recent illness. Would like a regular appointment with facility's beautician. She always uses a dandruff shampoo — her daughter will furnish it.

Likes to take a tub bath daily about 10 p.m. so she can "relax and fall asleep." Uses bath oil to alleviate "usual" dry skin. Occasionally gets up at night to go to bathroom and has no trouble returning to sleep. Usually retires after Johnny Carson show and arises at 6 a.m. Reads bible before breakfast.

Does not exercise regularly — tires easily. Has been independent in ADL's. Good appetite. Complains of blurring vision for last 6 months. Wears bifocal glasses. Has not seen her opthomologist since January 1976 and would like to continue seeing him.

Wears full dentures, last saw dentist for denture relining July 1978.

Learned to do breast self-exam 6 years ago and remembers to do it monthly.

Complains of stiffness in hands and knees in morning which goes away with mild exercise. Mild ankle edema.

Has been constipated "many" years and regularly uses milk of magnesia.

Carolyn Benoit, RN	8-14-78
Signature of person completing form	Date

NURSING HISTORY   Page 2 of 2

NURSING ASSESSMENT

ELEMENTS OF ASSESSMENT / DATE OF ASSESSMENT	8/11/78								
GENERAL APPEARANCE	0								

0. Clean-Neat-Well Groomed
1. Clean-Untidy Re: Grooming
2. Odor
3. Soils Self and Clothing

SKIN INTEGRITY	39								

0. Intact
1. Dry
2. Healed Decubitus (locate_____)
3. Varicosities
4. Hemorrhoids
5. Rash
6. Discoloration
7. Incision: Not Healed
8. Cyst
9. Open Area

SCALP	0								

0. No Open Area, Hair Clean, No Crust
1. Dandruff
2. Moderate Crusting
3. Heavily Crusted
4. Cyst
5. Open Area

ORAL CAVITY	0								

0. Mucosa Pink Moist - No Open Areas
1. Coated Tongue
2. Swollen Gums
3. Discolored Tissue
4. Bleeding Gums
5. Halitosis
6. Lesion (Open or Unopen)
7. Tonsillar Hypertrophy
8. Drainage

DENTITION	1								

0. Own teeth adequate to chew meat
1. Teeth absent but compensated, can chew meat
2. Dentures fit poorly, difficult to chew meat
3. Refuses to wear dentures
4. Teeth absent and not compensated, cannot chew meat
5. Heavy plaque or tartar on teeth
6. Teeth present, numerous caries

HEARING	0								

0. Can hear normal conversation
1. Impaired and corrected to hear normal conversation
2. Ringing or buzzing
3. Wax plugs
4. Impaired and not corrected to hear normal conversation
5. Refuses to wear hearing aid

VISION	12								

0. Functional
1. Impaired and corrected
2. Cannot read small print
3. Impaired and not corrected, dependent with all ADL's
4. Visual field cut
5. Extraocular movements (poor tracking)
6. Blind
7. Abnormal eye structure (Type _____)

PATIENT NAME *Johnson, Marie*   MED REC NO. **68495**

NURSING ASSESSMENT

Form 404

R.O.M.: SHOULDER, ARM, HAND	O								

0. Full range
1. Limited range
2. Partial ADL's capacity

3. Severely limited range, unable to perform ADL's
4. Contracture (locate _____)

R.O.M.: HIP, LEG AND FOOT	O								

0. Full range
1. Limited range
2. Partial ADL's capacity

3. Severely limited range, unable to perform ADL's
4. Contracture (locate _____)

CONDITION OF FEET	07								

0. Normal color, shape, temp., sensation
1. Thick or long nails
2. Discoloration
3. C/O cold or cold to touch
4. Malformed: special shoes

5. Malformed: poorly fitting shoes
6. C/O pain or poor sensation to pain stimulus
7. Corn or callus
8. Bunion
9. Open area

NEURO-MUSCULOSKELETAL	O								

0. Normal grip, resistive R.O.M., coordination, posture, balance
1. Weak - poor resistive R.O.M.
2. Poor posture

3. Poor spatial perception
4. Poor coordination or balance
5. Paralysis (location: _____)

TOUCH SENSATION	O								

0. Can feel touch, hot, cold, sharp, pain, smooth, rough
1. Cannot feel smooth
2. Cannot feel rough
3. Cannot feel sharp

4. Cannot feel cold
5. Cannot feel hot
6. Cannot feel touch
7. Cannot feel pain

CIRCULATION	05								

0. Pink, warm, full sensation in hands and feet, pedal pulses present and equal
1. Discolored
2. Healed statis ulcer
3. Poor sensation hands or feet

4. Cool to touch
5. Mild edema
6. Pedal pulse absent
7. Stasis ulcer
8. Pitting edema

ELIMINATION: BOWEL	O								

0. Continent, normal formed stool
1. Occasional impaction
2. Occasional loose stools
3. Occasional incontinence

4. Incontinent, candidate for retraining
5. Incontinent, not candidate for retraining
6. Ostomy
7. Abnormal stool characteristics

ELIMINATION: BLADDER	O								

0. Continent, normal amount and characteristics of urine
1. Dribbles
2. Occasional incontinence
3. Incontinent at night

4. Incontinent, candidate for retraining
5. Incontinent, not candidate for retraining
6. Ostomy
7. Catheter
8. Three or more urinary tract infections in past 12 months

HYDRATION	l								

0. Adequate fluid intake independently, good skin turgor
1. Adequate fluid intake with help or encouragement

2. Poor fluid intake
3. Poor skin turgor
4. Longitudinal wrinkles and furrows of tongue
5. Soft eyeballs

NUTRITION: BEHAVIORS	07								

0. No problem eating or feeding self, consumes at least ¾ of all foods served
1. Forgets mealtime
2. Snacks between meals, does not eat ¾ of all foods served
3. Cannot feed self independently
4. Frequently refuses meals
5. Frequently refuses same category of food
6. Chronic diarrhea
7. Chronic constipation or impactions
8. Chronic indigestion
9. Difficulty swallowing

NUTRITION: PROBLEM INDICATORS	56								

0. Hgb. normal, wt. within normal range for age and height, pink moist mucus membranes, shiny hair
1. No hgb. report
2. Hgb. more than 1 year old
3. Dull dry hair
4. Pallor of conjunctiva and palms
5. Low hgb.
6. Overweight for age and height
7. Underweight for age and height
8. Glossitis
9. Sores on lips or oral cavity

RESPIRATION	O								

0. Absence of respiratory difficulty, normal color, tolerates moderate exertion
1. Dyspnea on exertion
2. Chronic cough
3. Expectorates
4. Dyspnea at rest
5. Cyanosis

VITAL SIGNS	125								

0. Within normal range
1. Systolic B.P. usually 160 or greater
2. Diastolic B.P. usually 90 or greater
3. Pulse frequently below 60
4. Pulse frequently above 90
5. Frequent low grade temps
6. Respiration usually greater than 24

ACTIVITY TOLERANCE	1								

0. Tolerates normal exertion, no dyspnea, no fatigue
1. Tires easily, no interference in capacity to perform ADL's
2. Requires rest period during ADL's

SLEEP: REST	04								

0. Feels rested
1. Awake at night once a week
2. Naps during day
3. Difficulty falling asleep
4. Awake at night more than once a week
5. Has trouble awakening

CONSCIOUSNESS	O								

0. Alert, responsive (verbal and reflex)
1. Lethargic, responsive (verbal and reflex)
2. Coma, non-responsive

COMMUNICATION ABILITY	O								

0. Can speak and comprehend conversation and writing
1. Cannot verbalize
2. Cannot use signs or gestures
3. Cannot write meaningfully
4. Cannot comprehend conversation
5. Cannot comprehend signs or gestures
6. Cannot comprehend writing
7. Language barrier (identify _____)

COGNITION	O								

0. Attentive, appropriate responses, initiates conversation
1. Usually attentive
2. Occasional inappropriate response
3. Inattentive
4. Inappropriate responses

ORIENTATION	O								

0. Oriented to person, place and time
1. Disoriented to person
2. Disoriented to place
3. Disoriented to time

PATIENT NAME Johnson, Marie	MED REC NO. 68495

NURSING ASSESSMENT

DECISION MAKING	O								

0. Takes initiative and makes life style choices
1. Makes life style choices when asked

2. Prefers not to make life style choices
3. Does not make life style choices

ADJUSTMENT TO HEALTH PROBLEMS	1456								

0. Acceptance
1. Lack of knowledge or understanding
2. Sad
3. "Bargaining"

4. Anger, anxiety, frustration
5. Fear
6. Denial or disbelief
7. Prolonged grieving

MORALE	O								

0. Participates in care program, adjusts to new situations, feels useful & needed
1. Expresses loneliness
2. Sad, does not feel needed

3. Does not participate in care program
4. Feels life isn't worth living
5. Withdrawn

INTERPERSONAL RELATIONSHIPS	O								

0. Contentment re: quality & frequency of communication with friends or family; initiates socialization with staff and patients
1. Discontentment re: quality & frequency of communication with friends or family

2. Does not initiate, but responds to socialization initiated by others
3. Frequently exhibits agitated behavior toward others
4. Does not respond to socialization initiated by others

EXERCISE	234								

0. Active, walks to all meals & activities
1. Active within mobility limits
2. Does not participate in exercise program

3. Does not walk out of doors regularly
4. Occasionally walks to meals or activities
5. Does not walk to meals or activities

ENVIRONMENT	O								

0. Compatible with roommate, has personal articles in living area, satisfied with room arrangement, clean belongings
1. Does not keep personal belongings clean

2. Does not have personal articles in living area
3. Dissatisfied with room arrangement
4. Does not feel compatible with roommate

Signature of nurse
completing assessment

1   Carolyn Benoit, RN

2

3

4

5

6

7

8

FUNCTIONAL ASSESSMENT
MOBILITY & DEXTERITY

DATE: 8/14/78

ACTIVITY	Status	Mark		ACTIVITY	Status	Mark
Turn in Bed	I	■		Wash (Hands, Face)	I	■
	A	☐			A	☐
	U	☐			U	☐
Lying to Standing	I	■		Brush Teeth	I	■
	A	☐			A	☐
	U	☐			U	☐
Sitting to Standing	I	■		Make up, Shave	I	■
	A	☐			A	☐
	U	☐			U	☐
Transfer (Wheel-Chair)	I	☐		Comb Hair	I	■
	A	☐			A	☐
	U	☐			U	☐
Transfer (Toilet)	I	■		Dress, Shirt on	I	■
	A	☐			A	☐
	U	☐			U	☐
Propel Wheelchair	I	☐		Dress, Shirt off	I	■
	A	☐			A	☐
	U	☐			U	☐
Feeding	I	■		Buttons, Zippers	I	■
	A	☐			A	☐
	U	☐			U	☐

I = Independent - green   A = Assistance - blue   U = Unable - red

PATIENT NAME: Johnson, Marie   MED REC NO. 68495

FUNCTIONAL ASSESSMENT
MOBILITY & DEXTERITY

Form 405

Task	I	A	U
Trousers, Pants on	■ □ □ □ □ □ □ □	□ □ □ □ □ □ □ □	□ □ □ □ □ □ □ □
Trousers, Pants Off	■ □ □ □ □ □ □ □	□ □ □ □ □ □ □ □	□ □ □ □ □ □ □ □
Stockings	■ □ □ □ □ □ □ □	□ □ □ □ □ □ □ □	□ □ □ □ □ □ □ □
Shoes On	■ □ □ □ □ □ □ □	□ □ □ □ □ □ □ □	□ □ □ □ □ □ □ □
Shoes Off	■ □ □ □ □ □ □ □	□ □ □ □ □ □ □ □	□ □ □ □ □ □ □ □
Shoes Fasten	■ □ □ □ □ □ □ □	□ □ □ □ □ □ □ □	□ □ □ □ □ □ □ □
Walk Outdoors	■ □ □ □ □ □ □ □	□ □ □ □ □ □ □ □	□ □ □ □ □ □ □ □
Walk Indoors	■ □ □ □ □ □ □ □	□ □ □ □ □ □ □ □	□ □ □ □ □ □ □ □
Stairs	■ □ □ □ □ □ □ □	□ □ □ □ □ □ □ □	□ □ □ □ □ □ □ □
Armsling	□ □ □ □ □ □ □ □	□ □ □ □ □ □ □ □	□ □ □ □ □ □ □ □
Brace	□ □ □ □ □ □ □ □	□ □ □ □ □ □ □ □	□ □ □ □ □ □ □ □
Use Telephone	■ □ □ □ □ □ □ □	□ □ □ □ □ □ □ □	□ □ □ □ □ □ □ □
Write Name	■ □ □ □ □ □ □ □	□ □ □ □ □ □ □ □	□ □ □ □ □ □ □ □

Signature of person completing functional assessment to be entered on following lines.

1 M. Brown, N.A.
2
3
4
5
6
7
8
9

85

NUTRITIONAL HISTORY & INITIAL ASSESSMENT

CHART INFORMATION

Date of Birth __5-9-08__   Sex ___ M __✓__ F   Admission Date __8-11-78__

Height __5'3"__   Weight __169__   Admitted From __Midway Hospital__

Ideal Weight __140__   Recent Weight Gain or Loss? __Gain gradual__   Amount? __20#__   Blood Pressure __160/92__
__Past 18 Mths__

SIGNIFICANT LABORATORY FINDINGS

Date	Test	Result	Normal	Date	Test	Result	Normal
8-8-78	FBS	118	(80-120)		BUN		(8-18)
	Sodium		(134-144)		Hemoglobin		(14-18 Male)
	Potassium		(3.5-5.5)	8-9-78	Hemoglobin	10.9	(12-16 Female)

SIGNIFICANT OBSERVATIONS

Usual urine glucose: Negative __✓__   Variable _____

Is edema visible? __Yes__   Where? __Ankle__   If so, are weekly weights recorded? __Yes__

Is Insulin used? __No__   Type and frequency _____

Oral hypoglycemics? __No__   Trade name and frequency _____

Diuretic ordered? __Yes__   Trade name and frequency __Esidrix - 50 mg bid__

Is Potassium supplement ordered? __No__

List Significant Medical Diagnoses: __Hypertension, Diverticulitis, Obesity, Rectal bleeding__

Describe any recent major surgery, illness, injury (in last 3 months):

Diet Ordered __1200 Calories, 3-5 gm Na, Fiber Restricted, Force Fluids.__

Has diet order been changed recently? (Describe) __Yes, hi Fiber diet normally recommended was changed to Fiber Restricted during diverticulitis flare-up. Calorie restriction is new.__

Person recording this data __A. Smith, DSS__   Date __8-15-78__

PATIENT INTERVIEW

Person Interviewed __Patient.__

Brief description of former food patterns, eating habits, food preferences, fads, etc.
__Generally eats a balanced variety of foods. Snacks frequently. Does not consume fluids well. Sometimes uses salt.__

Are these food groups seldom or never eaten? Milk _____ Dairy _____ Eggs _____

Meat _____ Fish __✓__ Fruits _____ Vegetables __✓__ Bread & Cereal _____

Why Not? __Dislikes fish. is afraid to eat raw vegetables. Is not fond of most cooked vegetables.__

PATIENT NAME __Johnson, Marie__   MED REC NO. __68495__

NUTRITIONAL HISTORY & INITIAL ASSESSMENT

Form 406

PATIENT INTERVIEW (continued)

Food Habits: (check box)   EATS WELL ☐   ENJOYS FOOD ☑   FINICKY APPETITE ☐

SKIPS MEALS ☐   FREQUENT SNACKS ☑   EATS RESTRICTED FOODS REGULARLY ☐

Does patient understand modified diet restrictions? _Needs further instruction_

List food allergies: _None_   List strong religious or cultural preferences:

Dental Status: Dentures? _Yes_   Do they fit? _Yes_   Are they used? _Yes_

General Physical Status:

	Normal	Deficit	Compensated
SPEECH	✓		
HEARING	✓		
SIGHT		✓	✓

Mental Status: Oriented? _Yes O.K_

Person recording this data _A. Smith D.S.S._   Date _8-15-78_

OBSERVATION OF FOOD CONSUMPTION

Dining Location? _Prefers own Room_

Estimate of actual food consumed:

Meal Time   Between Meal Nourishments

Leaves a part of Vegetable Serving   _Likes her H.S. Snack_
Eats everything else on tray

Eating capability: Must be fed _____ Needs help _____ Feeds self _✓_

Person recording this data _A. Smith D.S.S._   Date _8-16-78_

CONCLUSIONS OF DIETITIAN OR DIETARY REPRESENTATIVE

Identify Problem Areas : _Overweight by approximately 30 pounds._
Hypertensive
Constipation

Suggestions to Improve Nutritional Intake:
1. _Control calories to aid weight loss._
2. _Re-instruct pt. on foods to avoid for high Sodium content._
3. _Provide vegetable juice as part of daily fluid intake._

Goal of Nutritional Care:
1. _Mrs. Johnson will lose weight at rate of 1-2 pounds per week until ideal weight (140#) is reached._
2. _Hemoglobin will be raised to normal range._
3. _Achieve adherence to 3-5 gm Na. restriction._

Person recording this data _J. Hesselman, R.D._   Date _8-18-78_

Date of Next Review _11-15-78_

This history and assessment form is based on the work of several experts and incorporates portions of assessment tools they have developed. It is used with their permission and that of their respective publishers. They are:

Overs, Robert P., et al., **Avocational Counseling Manual: A Complete Guide to Leisure Guidance.** Washington, D.C., Hawkins and Associates Incorporated, 1977.

THERAPEUTIC RECREATION

Birthdate: *May 9, 1908* Birthplace: *Sussey, Wisc.*

ADMISSION DATE *8 - 11 - 78*

Education: 1 2 3 4 5 6 7 8 9 10 11 (12)

Additional Education: *none* Specify Vocation: *Secretary 3M Co., homemaker*

Language Spoken: (English) - Other: _____

Interview Informant: (Patient) - Other: _____ Specify

LEISURE PATTERNS AND STYLES:

In 1927, Marie Johnson married Nels, a physician, and reared their 2 children while living in St. Paul. They lived there until 1972 and became actively involved with the Trinity Lutheran Church. For five (5) years she played the piano for Sunday school and sang in the church choir. She was a member of a local gardening club called "The Gardeneers" and has won several awards for her canned tomatoes, green beans, and carrots at the Minnesota State Fair. She continues to enjoy potted plants and has two African Violets and a Boston Fern in her room. Their family has enjoyed vacationing in the Black Hills of South Dakota, periodic summer fishing trips to Mille Lacs, Mn., and the Grand Canyon. Prior to her hospitalization, she enjoyed listening to the radio in the a.m., and watching T.V. She never misses Lawrence Welk. She also reads the Bible, religious literature, and newspapers regularly, and visits with neighbors fairly frequently. She is interested in participating in the facility's Protestant services although she expressed a desire to occasionally attend services at Trinity Lutheran. When asked if she would like to join a Golden Age club and attend monthly meetings she said "Fine, when I get my strength back." She dislikes handicrafts, and has played cards, ie., bridge, 500, Whist, Sin, as well as Bingo and competitive bowling.

PATIENT NAME
Johnson, Marie

MED. REC. NO.
68495

LEISURE HISTORY AND ASSESSMENT

Form 401

Avedon, Elliott M., **Therapeutic Recreation Service: An Applied Behavior Science Approach.** Englewood Cliffs, N.J., Prentice-Hall, Inc., 1974.

"Communications Status Chart," developed by Janice D. Stovall, Chief, Section of Patient Care Practices, Division of Health, Department of Health and Social Services, State of Wisconsin, Madison, Wisconsin. (Personal communication.)

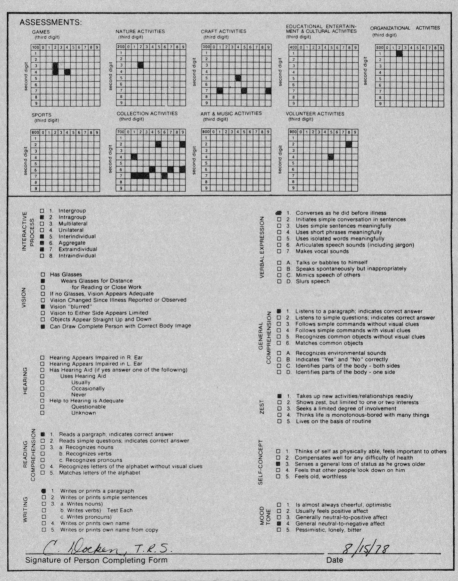

SOCIAL HISTORY

ADMISSION DATE
8-11-78

Mrs. Johnson was born May 9, 1908 and raised in a small town in Wisconsin. Her father owned and operated a small community cheese factory. Her mother helped out with the factory's bookkeeping. Mrs. Johnson had an older sister and a younger brother and sister. She describes her family relationships as "typically happy."

Mrs. Johnson graduated from high school and took a secretarial job in Minneapolis shortly thereafter. She was married in 1927 to Nels Johnson, a physician in St. Paul. Except for the first few years of Dr. Johnson's practice, they have had a very comfortable financial status. They had two children: Mike, the oldest, who is a practicing physician in Minneapolis and Carol, who is a trained physical therapist, and lives with her husband and family in Prior Lake.

Because of her husband's practice, she had little assistance raising the children and took on considerable entertaining and social responsibilities. She verbalizes pride in her prior independence and feels that the child rearing years forced her to become quite self-sufficient. She describes her relationship with her husband as "comfortable." Although proud of his accomplishments, she does not report more intimate feelings until describing their years together after his retirement in 1955, when she feels they began to "live." They traveled extensively and "carried on the good life" until her husband's health deteriorated.

In 1970 Mr. Johnson was diagnosed as having lung cancer. Mrs. Johnson cared for him in their home for the duration of his life with the exception of his last few months. She describes his death as "painful, loving and very emotionally trying." Perhaps because of this experience she appears to be abnormally sensitive to cancer symptoms. She expresses the fear that she too is suffering from cancer, and that her family and doctor are lying to her about her diagnosis.

In 1972 Mrs. Johnson sold the family home and moved into a senior citizen high rise. She states her children wanted her to move in with them but she refused, believing that both she and her children ought to be independent. She expresses a fear of becoming dependent on her children. She continued many of her civic and religious activities until 1977 when her health began to fail. Because of medical problems described elsewhere in this chart, Mrs. Johnson has in the last few months totally

Signature of person completing form   Date

PATIENT NAME Johnson, Marie   MED REC NO. 68495

SOCIAL HISTORY

Page 1 of 2

Form 402

ADMISSION DATE
8-11-78

restricted her outside contacts. If it were not for her supportive son and daughter who visited her quite regularly she probably would have become a total recluse.

Mrs. Johnson is oriented to person, place and time and is able to express herself quite adequately. She is anxious but outwardly acts optomistic about recovery. Her goal is to return to independent living. Mrs. Johnson verbalizes a desire to do whatever is necessary to get well and be discharged.

Social Services Assessment

Pre-admission visit: Mrs. Johnson stated during a pre-admission visit that she has accepted the need for nursing home placement but is fearful that she is going there to "die of cancer." She appeared interested in photos of the facility and suggested that if she is given time, she would become accustomed to her new surroundings.

Mrs. Johnson has considerable pride and ego strength. She She strongly needs to preserve her independence and self-determination. She will likely have difficulty adjusting to institutional life. The staff should encourage social participation but not be pushy. She is concerned with controlling her environment while at the same time maintaining her high social standards. Her belief that she actually has cancer is causing a high level of anxiety and nervousness. The social service department will continue to counsel with her weekly to: 1) allow ventilation of anxious feelings; 2) help orient her to new environment and work through relocation trauma; 3) establish a trust relationship which will enable her to accept her true medical condition and be comfortable with limited dependence on family and staff.

Margaret A. McManus, MSW	Aug. 15, 1978
Signature of person completing form	Date

PROBLEM/NEED LIST

NUMBER	DISEASE INDEX CARD NO.	ACTIVE PROBLEM/NEED	DATE OF ONSET	DATE INACTIVE
1	562.1 564.0	Mild diverticulosis with chronic constipation	1965	
2	562.1 569.2	Resolving diverticulitis, secondary to #1 with rectal bleeding	July 1978	
3		Blood loss anemia secondary to #2	July '78	
4	918	Excoriated skin in perianal area secondary to #2	7/6/78	
5	401	Hypertension with intermittent mild edema	1975	
6	277	Obesity	1976	
7	300.0	Mild anxiety secondary to #2 a) fear of cancer	July 1978	
8	374.9	Immature bilateral cataracts	Feb '78	
9	454.9	Varicosities, both legs	P.T.A.	
10	525.0	Edentulous	PTA	
11		Corns and callouses, both feet	PTA	
12	713.0	Osteoarthritis a) knees b) hands	PTA	
13		Expresses fear of dependence	7/11/78	
14		Primary health needs		
15		Expressed need to continue former leisure patterns and activities	7/15/78	
16		Expresses need for spiritual counseling	7/15/78	
17		Life-style preferences		

PATIENT NAME Johnson, Marie

MED REC NO. 68495

Form 452

ACUTE SELF-LIMITING PROBLEMS (TEMPORARY)

PROBLEM NO.	PROBLEM	DATES OF OCCURANCES					
		1	2	3	4	5	6
A	Head cold	5/21					
B	Crying jag	5/22					
C							
D							
E							
F							
G							
H							
I							
J							
K							
L							
M							

ACUTE SELF-LIMITING PROBLEMS (TEMPORARY)

MASTER HEALTH CARE PLAN

DATE OF CONFERENCE 8/17/78

REHABILITATION POTENTIAL *Excellent for discharge and return to independent living due to anticipated weight loss and healing of diverticulitis.*

DISCHARGE PLAN *When goals are attained and weight has decreased to 140#, consider discharge to prior residence with appropriate community resource support.*

NO.	DATE OF ONSET	PROBLEMS/NEEDS AND EXPECTED OUTCOMES	PLAN (Dx, Rx, Ed)	ACCOUNT-ABILITY
1	1965	Mild diverticulosis with chronic constipation	Dx: Observe stool consistency + frequency	NA
			Rx: Exercise program qd x 30 min. Check	TR
		Expected Outcome: Establish	pulse q̄ 10 min/stop if > 90 bpm.	*NA
		soft stools	Colace 100 mg qd in a.m. / PRN	CN
			Force fluids to 2000 cc's/day	NA
			Ed: Explain importance of regular bowel	
			evacuation, fluids and exercise.	CN
2	July 1978	Resolving diverticulitis secondary to #1 with rectal bleeding.	Dx: Observe stool for blood	NA
			Stool guaiac x 3 consecutive bm's	CN
			Rx: Achromycin (O) 250 mg qid x 21 days	
		Expected Outcome: Eliminate infection and bleeding.	2 hrs. a.c. meals	CN
			Fiber restricted diet	DSS
			Ed: Explain reasons for meds, lab tests,	
			and restricted diet; ask pt. to call	
			nurse to check bm's.	CN
3	July 1978	Blood loss anemia	Dx: Hgb q̄ month.	CN
		Expected Outcome: Establish	Rx: Feosol spansule, 1 cap. bid	
		hgb >12	x 1 month c̄ meals.	CN
			Ed: Explain reasons for meds, lab tests	CN
4	8/6 1978	Excoriated skin in perianal area, secondary to #2.	Dx: Observe qd for changes in	
			size and degree of excoriation.	CN
		Expected Outcome: Clear excoriation.	Rx: Cleanse p̄ bm's & at h.s. c̄	CN
			mild soap & apply bacimycin to	
			excoriated area	
			Ed: Instruct pt. re: importance	
			of skin care p̄ bm's.	CN
		(continued on back)		

PATIENT NAME Johnson, Marie

MED REC NO. 68495

MASTER HEALTH CARE PLAN

Form 453

NO.	DATE OF ONSET	PROBLEMS/NEEDS AND EXPECTED OUTCOMES	PLAN (Dx, Rx, Ed)	ACCOUNT-ABILITY
5	1975	Hypertension c̄ intermittent mild ankle edema.	Dx: BP q̄ a.m. Ⓡ arm; call M.D. if >180/100.	CN
		Expected Outcome: Control BP to <150/90 and eliminate ankle edema.	Check ankle edema q̄ d; notify M.O. if >2+	CN
			Rx: Esidrix (O) 50 mg, 1 tab. bid	CN
			3-5 gm Na diet	DSS
			Elevate feet 30 min. bid/PRN	NA/TR
			Ed: Explain reasons for Na-restricted diet & elevation of feet.	DSS/CN
			Explain diet restrictions to family & discourage bringing in restricted food.	SW
6	1976	Obesity	Dx: Weigh q̄ Monday ā breakfast	NA
		Expected Outcome: Reduce wt. to 140# at rate of 1-2#/week	Observe between meal eating.	AS
			Rx: 1200 cal. diet.	DSS
			Multivitamin c̄ trace minerals, 1 cap a.m.	• CN
			Slimnastics club.	DSS/TR
			Ed: Explain relationship of excess wt. to elevated BP, and importance of following 1200 cal diet c̄ no high cal. snacks.	CN/DSS
7	July 1978	Mild anxiety secondary to #2	Dx: Check c̄ MD re sharing medical info c̄ patient.	CN
		a) fear of cancer	Rx: Valium 10 mg bid/PRN	CN
		Expected Outcome: Will voluntarily express belief in real nature of problem c̄ no indication of anxiety, by ceasing to swear at and strike residents and staff	Daily 1:1 counseling to establish relationship of trust.	SW
			Passive friendliness by all staff; wait for pt. to make first move & respond accordingly.	AS
			Ed: Review/show medical record to pt. (c̄ MD's approval) to promote understanding and allay fears.	CN

NO.	DATE OF ONSET	PROBLEMS/NEEDS AND EXPECTED OUTCOMES	PLAN (Dx, Rx, Ed)	ACCOUNT-ABILITY
8	Feb. 1978	Immature bilateral cataracts.	Dx; Schedule eye exam c̄ ophthalmologist ASAP	CN
		Expected Outcome: Maintain independence in ADLs with the use of adaptive devices.	Rx: Contact family to obtain hi-intensity reading lamp & magnifying glass. Provide large-print Bible and telephone dial. Check out large-print newspaper from resident's library.	SW
				TR
			Ed: None	
9	PTA	Varicosities, both legs.	Dx: Check legs on bath day.	CN
		Expected Outcome: Prevent inflammation, stasis ulcer, and discomfort.	Rx: Support hosiery.	CN
			Elevate feet whenever possible.	NA
			Elevate foot of bed at night.	CN
			Ed: Instruct in avoiding tight garters, crossing legs, prolonged standing or sitting, importance of reduced weight & correct procedure for putting on support hose.	CN
10	PTA	Edentulous	Dx: Check c̄ pt. weekly about sore or tender gums.	CN
		Expected Outcome: Maintain ability to chew meat.	Rx: Full dentures.	
			Ed: Instruct in importance of reporting gum changes/denture problems promptly.	CN
11	PTA	Corns and callouses, both feet.	Dx: Schedule regular appt. c̄ podiatrist	CN
			Check type of footwear.	CN
		Expected Outcome: Eliminate corns and callouses.	Rx: Contact family to obtain soft shoes	SW
			Foot soak q̄ day.	NA
			Ed: None.	
12	PTA	Osteoarthritis a) knees and b) hands.	Dx: Check c̄ MD re OK for Aqua-K pad to knees PRN.	CN
		Expected Outcome: Maintain ADL independence and control discomfort.	Rx: AROM q̄ a.m.	NA
			ASA 10 gr PRN	CN
			Ed: Instruct re avoiding excessive exercise, including rest periods, & stopping exercise if painful. Instruct in relationship of excess weight to symptoms.	CN

MASTER HEALTH CARE PLAN

NO.	DATE OF ONSET	PROBLEMS/NEEDS AND EXPECTED OUTCOMES	PLAN (Dx, Rx, Ed)	ACCOUNT-ABILITY
13	8/11 1978	Expresses fear of becoming dependent. Expected Outcome: Will feel comfortable c̄ limited dependence by asking family + staff for assistance as necessary.	Dx: None Rx: 1:1 counseling to permit pt. to vent fears and work through problem Ed: None.	SW
14		Primary health needs. Expected Outcome: Maintain optimal health.	Dx: Pap smear in November, 1978 Self breast exam q month. Rx: Bivalent flu vaccine in October, 78 Ed: Review self breast exam techniques	CN CN CN
15	8/15 1978	Expresses need to continue former leisure patterns + styles. Expected Outcome: Voluntarily participates in activities of her choice.	Dx: None Rx: Gardening (vegetable) club, song fests, piano playing, TV (Waltons, L. wk.) Ed: None	TR
16	8/15 1978	Expresses need for continuing spiritual activities. Expected Outcome: Voluntarily participates in religious services of her choice.	Dx: None Rx: Notify pastor of pt.'s residence in nursing home. Have chaplain visit pt. q. week. Lutheran chapel services. Weekly visits by volunteers from Luth. women's circle. Ed: None	SW TR VC
17		Life-style preferences. Expected Outcome: Establish life-style patterns acceptable to patient. Participants: C. Benoit, R.N. G. Klocken, T.R.C. M. McManus, SW	Dx: None Rx: Weekly beauty shop appointment Evening tub bath c̄ bath oil Provision to watch late TV in dayroom H.S. Snack Ed: None A. Smith, DSS M. Brown, N.A. G. Heinz, V.C.	CN CN TR DSS/CN

MASTER HEALTH CARE PLAN

INTEGRATED PATIENT PROGRESS NOTES

DATE TIME	PROB DEPT	NOTES
8/11/78	NS	70 yr. old alert, oriented white female admitted ambulatory to
2 PM	Adm	116-2 accompanied by daughter. Nursing Assessment completed.
		T 99(o) P 80 reg. R 20 Wt. 169 Ht. 5'3" BP 160/92 (R) 156/90 (L) no known
		allergies. Skin pale, warm & moist. Excoriated 6 cm perianal area.
		Feet warm & dry, nails long. Corns & callous lateral aspect both
		feet. Varicosities inner aspect of both thighs & behind knees.
		Wears full snug dentures & can chew meat - no lesions in
		mouth. C/o blurred vision, wears bifocals. C/o chronic constipation.
		No meds brought in. Expresses concern over "bowel problems."
		States husband died of cancer & she knows "the symptoms." Becomes
		somewhat excited when discussing this problem. Wears yellow
		gold wedding band & yellow gold Timex watch. Mild bilateral
		ankle edema. Temporary nursing care plan:
		Diverticulitis → rectal bleeding
		Dx - observe all BM's
		Rx - achromycin
		Ed - instruct to call nurse to ✓ each BM
		Excoriated peri-anal area
		Dx - ✓ daily
		Rx - Cleanse p̄ BM & apply oint. as ordered
		Constipation
		Dx - observe freq. & characteristics
		Rx - collace, force fluids
		Hypertension c̄ ankle edema
		Dx - BP q̄d am (R) arm, call dr if > 180/100
		✓ ankle edema q̄d, call dr if > 2+
		Rx - 3-5 gm Na diet, esidrex
		Obesity
		Dx - Wt. q̄ Monday b4 breakfast
		Rx - 1200 cal. diet
		Anxiety
		Rx - Serax, spend time listening to her fears
		Explain reason every nursing action. C. Benoit, RN
8/11/78	DSS	Diet order for 1200 Calories, 3-5 gm-Na, fiber-restricted diet
3 PM	Adm	received and will implement. H.S. snack will be provided. A. Smith DSS

PATIENT NAME Johnson, Marie   **MED REC NO.** 68495

INTEGRATED PATIENT PROGRESS NOTES

Form 456

INTEGRATED PATIENT PROGRESS NOTES

DATE TIME	PROB DEPT	NOTES
8/11/78 3:30 PM	T.R. Adm	Introduced myself and identified my role. When asked if she preferred to be called by her sir or first name she replied, "Mrs. Johnson would be fine." I reviewed our TR scheduled program, resident council meetings, religious services and discussed the facility's resources, ie. library, music room, TV location and gave her a copy of the residents newspaper for her reference. I asked if she had any questions or requests to which she responded, "Yes, I'd like to go to church services on Sunday." I informed Mrs. Johnson of the time and location and will notify T.R., Nsg., and Clergy of her request. Upon concluding our conversation, I said I would return on Tuesday, A.M., to discuss her leisure interests in greater detail. — C. Docken, TRS
8/11/78 4 pm	SS Adm	Alert, aware she is in N.H. Somewhat anxious and apprehensive, prefers to eat meals in room and is more comfortable with one-to-one relationships. Dtr. very supportive and understanding. Consent forms and Bill of Rights explained to pt. who showed good comprehension and understanding. Pt. introduced to roommate and appropriate staff; given tour of facility. Asked questions, communicative with roommate and cooperative with staff. Pt. is aware that I am available to discuss problems or feelings which may arise. M. McManus, SW
8/11/78 6 PM	NS	T. 99 (o) P 82 reg R 20 BP 160/90 Ate all of supper — which she prefers to eat in room. Alert + oriented, pleasant. S. Nelson, RN
8/11/78 10 PM	NS	T. 99² (o) P 82 reg R 20 BP 162/90 Spent evening chatting with roommate. Evening shower. Says she always showers before retiring. Requested + given cocoa at HS "so she can sleep." S. Nelson, RN
8/12/78 2 AM	NS	T 98⁸ P 78 reg R 16 BP 154/88 Alert + Oriented when awakened for vital signs. Voided. Had been sleeping soundly. M. O'Malley, R.N.
8/12/78 6 AM	NS	T 98⁴ P 76 reg. R 16 BP 154/88 Well rested. Pleasant + Cooperative. Independent in morning cares. Voided. M. O'Malley R.N.
8/12/78 10 A	NS	Ate all of breakfast except white toast.

PATIENT NAME Johnson, Marie

MED REC NO. 68495

INTEGRATED PATIENT PROGRESS NOTES

Form 456

INTEGRATED PATIENT PROGRESS NOTES

DATE TIME	PROB DEPT	NOTES
8/12/78 10 am	NS	Prefers dark bread + wishes to continue eating meals in room "for now." T 99 P 82 reg. R 20 BP 158/90 C. Benoit, RN
8/13/78 2 pm	NS	T 99(0) P 80 reg. R 20 BP 160/90 Spent most of day reading bible + chatting with roommate. Daughter brought in clothing and 2 African Violets. Would like to subscribe to St. Paul morning newspaper. C. Benoit, RN
8/17/78 1 PM	NS	Initial care planning conference held. C. Benoit, RN
8-18 1:30 pm	#2 Dietary	Resolving. Diverticulitis secondary to #1 S. "I like whole grain toast and bread. I want some and told the nurse several days ago. O. Whole grain breads not permitted on Fiber Restricted Diet A. Because of recent diet change from Hi-Fiber diet to Fiber-Restricted, she does not understand foods allowed. P. Dx - None Rx - Provide rye bread allowed. Ed. - Explain that this diet change is a temporary therapeutic measure for inflammation (dev) H. Smith, NSS
8/18/78 2 P.M.	#15 T.R.	Expresses need to continue former leisure patterns and styles. S - When gardening, pt. asked, "I really like this. Do you suppose I could plant some mums in another area of the yard?" O - Pt. has been weeding vegetable garden almost daily for the past week, generally for 15-20 minutes. A - Pt. enjoys tending the garden, and it does not appear to be too strenuous an activity for her. Additional gardening space probably would not over-tax her strength. P - Continue plan as developed. Ask maintenance to prepare flower bed by north wing - C. Daken, TRS
8/22/78 2:30 pm	B SS	Crying jag S - "I'm so worried. I know they're lying to me." O - In room alone crying. Stopped crying when I talked with her A - Fears that she has cancer and becomes more upset about it when feeling lonely

PATIENT NAME	Johnson, Marie	MED REC NO.	68495

INTEGRATED PATIENT PROGRESS NOTES

Form 456

INTEGRATED PATIENT PROGRESS NOTES

DATE TIME	PROB DEPT	NOTES
8/22/78	B	Crying jag (cont)
2:30 pm	SS	P - Continue 1:1 visits to reassure her about diagnosis and allow
		her to vent feelings; encourage participation in activities planned
		for her M. McManus, SW
8/24/78	#12	Expresses fear of dependence
1 pm	SS	S- "I think I'll stay with my daughter this weekend"
		O- Pt smiling and relaxed. Expresses fear of dependence less frequently
		A- Pt more comfortable about showing need for family
		P- Encourage visiting daughter, discuss visit with her M. McManus, SW

PATIENT NAME Johnson, Marie	MED REC NO. 68495

INTEGRATED PATIENT PROGRESS NOTES

Copyright Medallion Communications, Inc. 1978
All Rights Reserved

Form 456

FLOW SHEET

HEIGHT _5' 3"_

DATE	TEMP	PULSE	RESP	WT	B/P	BREAST EXAM	Hgb.	ANKLE EDEMA L	R	B.M. Consist.	Excor. cm.		
8-11-78 (2p)	99	80	20	169	160/92			1+	1+		6		
(6p)	99	82	20		160/90								
(10p)	99²	82	20		162/90								
8-12-78 (2A)	98⁸	78	16		156/88			1+	1+		6		
(6A)	98⁴	76	16		156/88								
(10A)	99	82	20		158/90					Hard Form			
(2p)	99	80	20		160/92								
8-13-78	98⁸				160/94			1+	1+		6		
8-14-78	98⁶			168	158/100			1+	1+	Hard Form	6		
8-15-78	98⁶				168/100			1+	1+		6		
8-16-78					158/92			1+	1+		5		
8-17-78					158/86			0	1+	Hard Form	5		
8-18-78					158/88			0	1+		5		
8-19-78					158/88			0	1+	Hard Form	4		
8-20-78					158/88			1+	1+		4		
8-21-78				167	156/88			1+	1+	Hard Form	4		

PATIENT NAME _Johnson, Marie_   MED REC NO. _68495_

FLOW SHEET

Appendix 2

Additional Patient Forms
(non-legal records)

HEALTH CARE PLAN CONFERENCE DATES.

LAST NAME Johnson FIRST Marie INT

REHAB. POTENTIAL Excellent for discharge and return to independent living due to anticipated weight loss and healing of diverticulitis.

DISCHARGE PLAN When goals are attained and weight has decreased to 140#, consider discharge to prior residence with appropriate community resource support.

Date of Onset	NO.	PROBLEM/NEED	EXPECTED OUTCOME	PLAN	Accountability
1965	1	Mild diverticulosis ē chronic constipation	Establish soft stools	Dx: Observe stool consistency ē frequency	NA
				Rx: Exercise Program ᵍd̄ x 20 min / check pulse ā 10 min / stop if > 90 bpm	TR/NA
				Colace 100 mg ᵍd in a.m. PRN	CN
				Force fluids to 2000 cc's/day	NA
				Ed: Explain importance of regular bowel evacuations, fluids, and exercise.	CN
July '78	2	Resolving diverticulitis secondary to #1, with rectal bleeding	Eliminate infection and bleeding	Dx: Observe stool for blood	NA
				Stool guaiac x 3 consecutive BM's	CN
				Rx: Achromycin (o) 250mg ᵍid x 21 days /2hrs ac meals	CN
				Fiber restricted diet	DSS
				Ed: Explain reasons for meds, lab tests, ↓ restricted diet; ask pt. to call nurse to check BM's.	CN
July '78	3	Blood loss anemia	Establish hgb >12	Dx: Hgb ā month	CN
				Rx: Feosol spansule, 1 cap. bid x 1 mouth ē meals	CN
				Ed: Explain reasons for meds, lab tests	CN
8/6/78	4	Excoriated skin in perianal area, secondary to #2	Clear excoriation	Dx: Observe ᵍd for changes in size and degree of excoriation	CN
				Rx: Cleanse p̄ BM's and at h.s. ē mild soap and apply bacimycin to excoriated area.	CN
				Ed: Instruct pt. re: importance of skin care p̄ BM's	CN
1975	5	Hypertension ē intermittent mild ankle edema	Control BP < 150/90 and eliminate ankle edema	Dx: BP ā a.m. / call M.D. if > 180/100	CN
				Rx: Esidrex (o) 50 mg, 1 tab. bid	CN
				3-5 gm Na diet	DSS
				Elevate feet 30 min. bid / PRN	NA/TR
				Ed: Explain reasons for Na-restricted diet and elevation of feet.	DSS/CN
				Explain diet restrictions to family and discourage bringing in restricted foods.	
1976	6	Obesity	Reduce weight to 140# at rate of 1-2 #/week	Dx: Weigh ā Monday ā breakfast	SW
				Observe between meal eating	NA
				Rx: 1200 Cal. diet	AS
				Multivitamin ē trace minerals, 1 cap. a.m.	DSS, CN

MONDAY	TUESDAY	WEDNESDAY	THURSDAY	FRIDAY	SATURDAY	SUNDAY
Weigh before breakfast 7 p.m. Song Fest	Hgb. ā month	Tub bath H.S. Clip toenails	Beauty Shop a.m. 10:30 Slimnastics Club	11 a.m. Exercise Group 2 p.m. Garden Club		10:30 Lutheran Church Services

Form 454

DIET: _1200 cal-5 fiber restricted_ 3-5 gm Na   DINING ROOM _BLD_   TRAY —

RESERVED FORM 455

ASSISTANCE NEEDED: _____

NOURISHMENTS: A.M. _120 cc o. juice_ P.M. _120 cc o. juice_ H.S. _120 cc o. juice_

FLUIDS _force_ to 2000 cc   I & O _____

SPECIAL REQUESTS _____

ALLERGIES

MEDICATION	FOOD	OTHER

MEDICATION

ORIG. ORDER DATE	MEDICATION	DOSE	ROUTE	FREQ	TIME	RENEW DATE	D/C DATE
8/11/78	Achromycin	250 mg	O	Q1D	6-10-4-8		8/31/78
8/11/78	Feosol Spansule	ĩ cap	O	BID	8-8		9/11/78
9/11/78	Multivitamin ĩ trace minerals	ĩ cap	O	A.M.	8		9/11/78
9/11/78	Esidrix	50 mg	O	BID	8-8		9/11/78

P.R.N. MEDICATIONS

8/11/78	Valium	10 mg	O	BID			9/11/78
9/11/78	Colace	100 mg	O	AM			9/11/78

H.S. MEDICATIONS

DOCTOR ORDERED TREATMENTS

DATE ORD	TREATMENT ORDERED	FREQ	TIME	D/C DATE
9/11/78	Bacitracin oint. to rectal area. Wash	5 BM. ĩ	HS	9/11/78
	skin ĩ mild soap before each application			
8/11/78	BP daily - call MD if > 180/100		a.m.	9/11/78
9/11/78	Hgb.		ĝ mo	9/11/78
9/11/78	Weigh		ĝ Monday	9/11/78
9/11/78	Observe stool for blood		a.c.	9/11/78
9/11/78	Observe ankle edema - call MD if > 2+			
9/11/78	Stool guaiac x 3 consecutive BMs			
9/11/78	Pap smear		Nov. 78	
8/11/78	Bivalent flu vaccine		Oct. 78	

L.O.A WITH MEDS: _Yes, up to 72 hours_

RESTRAINTS: _____

B.P. _160/90_   T.P.R. _99(0) - 82 - 20_   ADM WT _169_

NURSING HOME CASE # _1568_   MEDICARE NO. _471-62-7346 A_

PUBLIC ASSIS # _____   CO _____

CARE CLASSIFICATION _____   MORTICIAN _____

NEAREST RELATIVE _Mrs. Carol Anderson (dtr.)_
Prior Lake, MN   _447-9658_

EMERGENCY NOTIFICATION _Mrs. Carol Anderson_   (RELATIONSHIP)

BILLING INFORMATION _____

RELIGION _Lutheran_   CLERGY _Trinity Luth._   PHONE _642-7100_

	NAME	PHONE	LAST VIS.	TO BE SEEN
PODIATRIST	Dr. Amity	247-5522	3-78	9-78
DENTIST	Dr. Moriarity	871-4716	2-77	
EYE	Dr. Monahan	973-5312	10-76	9-78
OTHER				

ATTENDING PHYSICIAN: VISIT ĝ _30 days_   LAST RITES ____   VISIT DUE _9/11/78_

NAME _Mark Welbeing, M.D._   ADDRESS _Central Medical Bldg._   TELEPHONE _645-3489_

DIAGNOSES:
Resolving Diverticulitis ĩ rectal bleeding ĩ anemia.
Hypertension ĩ mild intermittent ankle edema.
Obesity   Constipation   Anxiety

ROOM	LAST NAME	FIRST	INITIAL	AGE	BIRTH DATE	ADM. DATE
104-2	Johnson	Marie		70	5-9-08	8-11-78

T.B. SCREENING

MANTOUX _O_   CHEST X-RAY _O_   DATE _8-8-78_

LAUNDRY: IN / OUT

S / W / (M) / D

COPYRIGHT© MEDALLION COMMUNICATIONS, INC. 1978 ALL RIGHTS

NOTE: Each team member completes a preparation worksheet prior to the team conference. The following worksheet, prepared by the Therapeutic recreation coordinator, exemplifies the process. Observe that the T.R. Coordinator has not confined her attention to the recreational and leisure needs, but has considered *all* of the patient's problems/needs.

PATIENT CARE CONFERENCE PREPARATION WORKSHEET

Expected outcome (goal) = Anticipated patient condition resulting from intervention

Dx = plans for gathering informations
Rx = plans for staff interventions
Ed = plans for patient or family education

Patient Name _Marie Johnson_
Admission Date _8/11/78_

DATA BASE SUMMARY	DATE OF ONSET	PROBLEM/NEED	EXPECTED OUTCOME	PLAN
70 y.o. old Mobility Lutheran Church - St. Paul 5 yrs. promo for S. School, Long in choir. Gardener - Garden Club - won awards, canned vegetables. Potted plants in room. Vacationing: Black Hills, Mo.?, Lakeshore resorts, Grand Canyon. TV, Lawrence Welk and radio. Bible & religious periodicals, newspaper daily, family photo album. Attended church regularly. Visit c̄ neighbors. 500, Whist, gin.	1974	Obesity	wt. to ___ lbs.	Dx: Weigh weekly Rx: Slimnastics Club (T.R.) c̄ (O.S.S.)
	1965	Constipation	est. soft stools	Rx: Exercise x 5 days a week (T.R.)
	1975	Hypertension	Control BP.	Rx: yoga - relaxation technique (T.R.) Ed: Explain importance of gaining a relaxed attitude toward life.
	PTA	Osteoarthritis	maintain good mobility and control discomfort	Rx: precaution - avoid (TR) strenuous & competitive sports and kicking games.
	PTA	Cataracts L & R	Maintain independence c̄ use of compensatory items	Dx: schedule dr. appt. Rx: large print books (TR) telephone dial, large print newspaper, in residents library.

DATA BASE SUMMARY	DATE OF ONSET	PROBLEM/NEED	EXPECTED OUTCOME	PLAN
Bingo, Bowling, Bakes crafts. Future: desires attendance at Trinity Church & activity & visit c̄ Chaplain. Interaction Patterns 2, 3, 6, 7 Vision, blurred Hearing, Verbal Exp., General Comp. Writing, Reading ok	8/11/78	Anxiety a) fear of cancer	Will express no fear of cancer.	Rx: Passive friendliness (AS) wards for pt to make first move & respond accordingly.
	8/11/78	Expressed desire to continue former leisure patterns & styles	Voluntarily participate in at least ? wk activities of her choice	Rx: vegetable garden-ing club, ping pong, bingo, piano playing, bowling, TV. (1 week) card club. Ed: describe location of TR calendar, schedule of events.
	8/11/78	Expressed desire to continue spiritual counseling	Voluntarily partici-pates in spiritual services of her choice	Rx: notify pastor (V.S.) of pt transfer to facility. Rev. Storey, Chaplain, visit pt. c̄ week. Lutheran & Roman Catholic. Cycle mag't c̄ wk Sunday Protestant Services.

Appendix 3

Planning Conference Evaluation Checklist

Health Care Planning Conference Evaluation Checklist

	YES	NO	COMMENT

WRITTEN PREPARATION

A. Data base is adequate re:

Medical History & Physical

Exam . . . . ___ ___ _____

Nursing Assessment . . . . ___ ___ _____

Nursing History . . . . ___ ___ _____

Functional Mobility & Dexterity

Assessment . . . . ___ ___ _____

Social History & Assessment . . . . . ___ ___ _____

Nutritional History & Initial

Assessment . . . . ___ ___ _____

Laboratory & X-ray Information . . ___ ___ _____

Environmental Assessment . . . . . . ___ ___ _____

Transfer Form . . . . ___ ___ _____

Leisure History & Assessment . . . ___ ___ _____

B. Preparation Worksheet completed

by all team members (except

Nurse Assistant and

Housekeeper . . . . ___ ___ _____

DOCUMENTATION

All problem/need areas were

addressed, including:

Active Diagnoses . . . . ___ ___ _____

Primary Health Needs . . . . ___ ___ _____

Functional Problems . . . . ___ ___ _____

Psychosocial Needs . . . . ___ ___ _____

Leisure Needs . . . . ___ ___ _____

Life-Style Preferences . . . . ___ ___ _____

Each problem/need on the problem

list is properly titled . . . . ___ ___ _____

Terminology is concise and accurate ___ ___ _____

Accountability is assigned . . . . ___ ___ _____

Expected outcomes are specified for

each problem/need . . . . ___ ___ _____

Restorative goals or expected out-

comes have a specific evaluation

date if appropriate . . . . ___ ___ _____

Recording is complete and con-

sistent with the manual, including:

110

	YES	NO	COMMENT
Rehabilitation Potential	__	__	_____
Initial Discharge Plan	__	__	_____
Dates of Onset for Each Problem/Need	__	__	_____
Dx, Rx and Ed are used according to Manual Definitions	__	__	_____
Signatures of all Conference Participants	__	__	_____

PARTICIPATION

All departments were represented . . .	__	__	_____
All team members were encouraged to participate	__	__	_____
All team members participated	__	__	_____
All team members attended entire meeting	__	__	_____

COMMUNICATION

Interpersonal rapport and openness were evident.	__	__	_____
Team members were patient oriented	__	__	_____
Discussion did not stray from the topic	__	__	_____
Attitudes reflected interest and enthusiasm	__	__	_____
No team members(s) dominated discussion.	__	__	_____
Team leader used blackboard effectively	__	__	_____
Team leader gave positive reinforcement	__	__	_____
Team leader guided group to purposeful completion of plan for each problem	__	__	_____
Verbal background summaries were brief	__	__	_____
Staff education needs were not addressed but noted for referral to Staff Development Coordinator	__	__	_____

Conference procedure was consist-
ent with the manual . . . . —   —   _____
All problems/needs were listed *prior*
to defining expected outcomes
and developing care plans . . . . —   —   _____
Channels used for communicating
plan to other shifts . . . .

MEETING ENVIRONMENT
Conference was held at scheduled
time and started promptly   —   —   _____
Conference was of appropriate
length . . . . —   —   _____
Conference held in comfortable and
adequate place . . . . —   —   _____
Conference was quiet and free from
interruptions . . . . —   —   _____

PATIENT/FAMILY INVOLVEMENT
Patient was present (if appropriate) . . —   —   _____
Patient participated in/was informed
of care planning . . . . —   —   _____
Plan was made for patient/family
conference . . . . —   —   _____

RECOMMENDATIONS FOR IMPROVING PATIENT CARE PLANNING
CONFERENCE: _____
_____
_____
_____
_____
_____
_____

COMPLETED BY:_____DATE:_____

Notes

Notes

Notes

Notes

118